ISBN 978-0-331-38545-8
PIBN 11115992

PREPARED FOR:

    WILKES COUNTY, NORTH CAROLINA

    BOARD OF COUNTY COMMISSIONERS
        James Spicer, Chairman, Millers Creek
        E. C. Eller, Jr., Ferguson
        Richard B. Johnston, North Wilkesboro
        Clyde R. Lowe, Moravian Falls
        Clifton Prevette, Roaring River

PREPARED BY: WILKES COUNTY PLANNING BOARD
        Charles Proffitt, Chairman, Boomer
        Charles Absher, Jr., Traphill
        Shalmer Blackburn, Route 1, Purlear
        John W. Bryan, Jr., Traphill
        Bryant Church, RFD 1, Wilkesboro
        John Dawson, Ferguson
        Robert H. McNeill, RFD 2, Wilkesboro
        David Parks, Box 4, Wilkesboro
        Vernon Triplett, Ferguson

TECHNICAL ASSISTANCE
PROVIDED BY:

    STATE OF NORTH CAROLINA
    DEPARTMENT OF CONSERVATION & DEVELOPMENT
    DIVISION OF COMMUNITY PLANNING
        George J. Monaghan, Administrator
    PIEDMONT AREA OFFICE
        Mathey A. Davis, Director
    PROJECT STAFF
        Robert C. Hinshaw, Project Planner*
        Paul L. Trexler, Draftsman
        G. Perry Whisnant, Draftsman
        M. Eileen Antosek, Stenographer

        *Responsible for this report

September, 1968   Price: $2.00

TABLE OF CONTENTS

MAPS

FIGURES

INTRODUCTION

Planning for a county, like planning for family or individual projects, is simply the wise use of foresight. Noting the potential for growth and development that has been realized since the time of the early settlers on the Yadkin River, Wilkes County officials have taken steps to guide this growth potential by planning for it.

Plans or studies for parts of Wilkes County that have already been published include: <u>A Geographical Study of Wilkes County</u>; <u>Population and Economy, Wilkes County</u>; and the <u>Zoning Ordinance of the W. Kerr Scott Reservoir Area</u>.* Several other plans have been produced for the Towns of Wilkesboro and North Wilkesboro, and subdivision regulations have been published for the entire county.

County officials recontracted with the North Carolina Department of Conservation and Development, Division of Community Planning, in March, 1967, for technical assistance in further planning work for the total Wilkes County area. This current effort will be completed by March, 1969, and will include the elements of Land Potential Study, Land Development Plan, and Public Facilities Plan. Also to be considered in this series will be further areas of zoning for the county.

This publication includes the first two elements -- the Land Potential Study and the Land Development Plan -- along with a brief summary of natural features found in the county. It will be noted that most of the maps and other graphics of this plan exclude detail around Wilkesboro and North Wilkesboro. This detail was omitted since it has been covered in depth by other publications from the Division of Community Planning for the area in and around the Wilkesboros.

With these elements completed, the way should be open for public improvements programs, capital improvements budgeting, and other private and public programs for implementing some of the plans and recommendations that have been made and will be made during the present planning efforts.

---

*
These publications were printed by the N. C. Department of Conservation and Development, Division of Community Planning, between the years of 1961 and 1964.

part 1

LOPMENT BACKGROUND

PART I

DEVELOPMENT BACKGROUND
AND NATURAL FEATURES

REGIONAL SETTING

The location and relation of Wilkes County to the rest of
North Carolina is shown by Map 1. Being some 765 square miles
in area, it is one of the largest counties in the State and has
land that is classified as being parts of both the Piedmont and
the Mountain sections of the three major North Carolina landform
regions.*

Wilkes County is near the northwestern corner of the State
where a tri-state junction is formed by North Carolina, Virginia
and Tennessee. Wilkes is bounded on the west and north sides by
the state boundary counties of Watauga, Ashe, Alleghany, and
Surry. Bordering the east and south are the counties of Yadkin,
Iredell, Alexander and Caldwell.

While Wilkes was among the lower density areas of population
in North Carolina in 1960, it is within easy driving reach of
many of the more urban population centers of the Piedmont. The
Town of North Wilkesboro, for example, is 79 miles north of
Charlotte, 54 miles west of Winston Salem, 82 miles west of
Greensboro, and 163 miles northwest of Raleigh.

There is no "trunk-line" air service nearer than Winston-
Salem, but there is a local airport that can handle aircraft as
large as the twin-engined "executive-type" planes and flights
are available to the larger city airports. This locates Wilkes
County by air less than two hours from New York City, Washington,
and Atlanta.

---
*The three general landform areas in North Carolina are the
Coastal Plain in the east, the Piedmont section in the central
portion, and the Mountain area in the west. The Geographical
Study of Wilkes County notes that much of the county is actually
a transitional zone where the landform areas change from the
lower, rolling Piedmont to the more rugged Appalachian Mountain
region.

HISTORICAL DEVELOPMENT

Recorded history of the Wilkes County area dates to at least 1753, when a white settler was found in the area by a Moravian bishop-surveyor.* It is not the purpose or intent of this present study to elaborate on the history of Wilkes County, but it is well to note at least the major factors that have brought about past growth and development. Some of the major historic events that relate to development are:

1774 Wilkes County formed from Surry County territory, with western boundary running roughly to the Mississippi River.

1775 County government organized.

1782 County developing into smaller farm pattern, compared with earlier large land grants. Average plantation size about 379 acres, with chief export of livestock. Horse ownership (over 92 per cent of families owning them) showed high standard of living compared to some counties in that day.

1788 Town of Wilkesboro organized as County Seat.

1850 Pre-Civil War population listed as 10,746 whites, 1,142 slaves, and 211 free Negroes.

1862-
1865 Second only to Mecklenburg County in number of men sent to Confederacy.

1891 Railway connection completed from Winston-Salem. Rails stopped across the Yadkin River from Wilkesboro, giving rise to the Town of North Wilkesboro.

1900 Industry, banking, and commerce beginning to grow fairly rapidly, based largely on lumber, wood products, and tanneries. Agriculture lagging from previous years. County population 15,549.

---

*Source: A New Geography of North Carolina, Vol II, Bill Sharpe, Sharpe Publishing Co., Raleigh, N.C., 1962

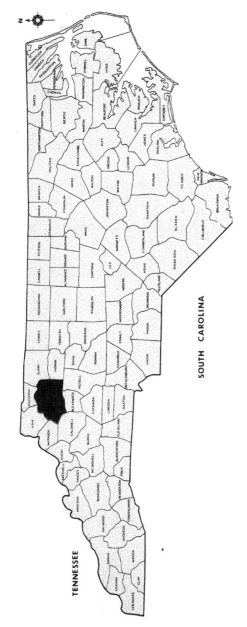

REGIONAL SETTING
WILKES COUNTY, NORTH CAROLINA

MAP-1

1910 Farming again on the increase with good range of small grains
     and export items of apples, vegetables, herbs, poultry and
     dairy products, nuts, and berries. Population of 30,282, with
     799 of these persons in Wilkesboro and 1,902 in North Wilkes-
     boro.

1916 County hard hit by a flood, bringing the death of 80 persons
     and much road and property damage.

1940 A second major flood with higher water and property damages
     than in 1916.

1954 Over 500,000 bushels of apples produced for sale. Poultry
     production increasing rapidly.

1960 Employment showing increases in manufacturing, commerce,
     and professional services -- agriculture declining. County
     population 45,269 persons, including 4,197 in North Wilkes-
     boro and 1,568 in Wilkesboro.

1962 W. Kerr Scott Reservoir completed on the Yadkin west of
     Wilkesboro, providing flood control, water supply, and
     recreation area.

1966 Agriculture still generally on decline except for poultry
     and livestock.

1967 Continued growth evident in retail and wholesale trade and
     in industry.

    Development in Wilkes County has changed radically from the
vast area and large landholders of its early years. It has become a county of smaller farms that tend to specialize in a few
crops or in livestock or poultry.

    While the agricultural scene was changing, the industrial,
commercial, and financial side of the picture has had favorable
gains except for some employment declines noted in more recent
years in declining or slow-growth industries.[*]

_____

[*]Source: Wilkes County Population and Economy, Division of
Community Planning, 1962

With at least 75 per cent of the County's 765 square miles
still in woods and much land virtually undeveloped, now is a good
time to be concerned with the planning of future growth and development. Planning and conservation of the many physical, economic,
and social resources can help shape the events that future residents of Wilkes County will look back on and call their history.

NATURAL FEATURES

Topography

The potential use and development of land in Wilkes County
is highly affected by the topography of this land. Aside from
the natural beauty of the mountains, their contours weigh heavily
in the factors that shape future growth.

Wilkes County has been described as a valley that is surround-
ed on three sides by mountains. These steep slopes provide natural
barriers to transportation, utility extensions, and other services
that people have come to consider highly important to places to
work and live. Even with modern earthmoving equipment and tech-
niques, much of the undeveloped part of the county is lost to any
form of intensive development at all except for scattered residences or vacation cottages. Areas included in this natural
barrier to development are shown on Map 2.

A brief analysis of the county via a topographic map reveals
that about 38 per cent of the total area is taken up by mountainous land with steep slopes. This amounts to some 290 square miles,
of the 765 total, that are not likely to be developed, not to
mention considerably more area that is not suitable for intensive
development due to the nearness to streams and topographic problems
that are not in the strictly mountainous areas. More details on
these areas will be included in the section on soils and geology.

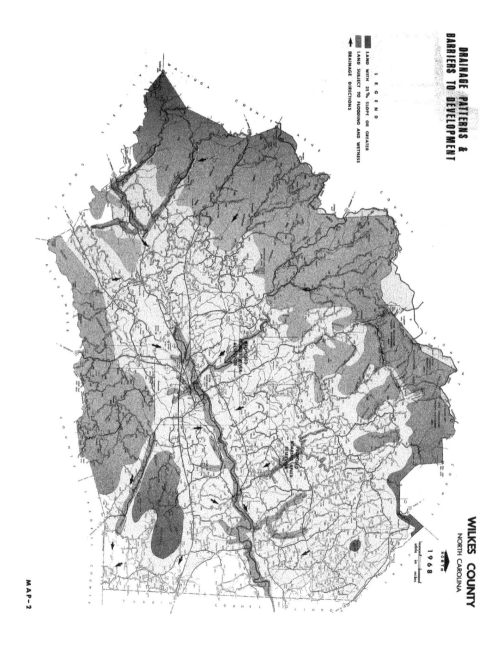

DRAINAGE PATTERNS &
BARRIERS TO DEVELOPMENT

L E G E N D

LAND WITH 25% SLOPE OR GREATER

LAND SUBJECT TO FLOODING AND WETNESS

DRAINAGE DIRECTIONS

WILKES COUNTY
NORTH CAROLINA

NORTH

1968

scale in miles

MAP-2

The geographic features of Wilkes County can be viewed in at least two ways. On one hand they offer scenic beauty and the related tourism and recreational potential that many areas can envy. The other point of view, however, is the fact that this same ruggedness will cause sizable portions of the land to be isolated or closed to urban use for at least the foreseeable future, i.e., the planning period of 1967 to 1990. Residents should therefore be reminded that at least one-half of their county is closed to further development due to topographic features and existing development.

Drainage Patterns

The primary drainage patterns for Wilkes County are also illustrated on Map 2. The general direction of surface water flow is of course from the mountains of the north, west, and south to the Yadkin River flowing diagonally across the lower center of the county. The only major exception to this direction of flow is in the southeastern corner of the county, where Hunting Creek and a few smaller streams flow in a southerly direction through the Brushy Mountains into Alexander, Iredell, or southern Yadkin County.

The W. Kerr Scott Reservoir, a Corps of Engineers project completed in 1962, has offered flood control to the Yadkin River Valley area west of Wilkesboro. Such major tributaries as the Reddies River and Roaring River further east, however, are still considered flood threats to eastern Wilkes County and land farther east.* The Reddies River Reservoir has been authorized as a U.S. Corps of Engineers project and study is being continued on the Roaring River project.** (Approximate coverage of the proposed reservoirs is shown on Map 2. While the land to be covered by water will be a "barrier" to development, these reservoirs should stimulate development within the immediate area surrounding them.)

_____
*
  Source: Flood Plain Information, Elkin and Jonesville, N.C.,
U.S. Corps of Engineers, Charleston, S. C., August, 1967
**Remarks by Jack F. Rasmussen, Chief, Planning Branch of U.S.
Army Engineer District, Charleston, S. C., before the Governor's
Appalachian Development Conference, Asheville, N.C., June 26, 1968

Water Resources

Water is generally available in good supply in Wilkes County both from surface and ground water sources. Both the Yadkin and Reddies Rivers were sources of water for the Wilkesboros in the past, and the W. Kerr Scott Reservoir is now the Wilkesboro reservoir. These sources have good potable water and are supplying the more heavily settled central portion of the county.

The water supply spreads into the more isolated portions of the county as well. Most farms, for example, have available streams or springs that make water for stock no problem. It will be noted in traveling through rural Wilkes County that most of the State-maintained roads cross streams numerous times, and except for an occasional thoughtless dumping of residential garbage, there are presently few sources of pollution.

There is obviously much interest in preserving the good water supply and in making the most of available sources. Studies are being completed and sites have been selected for dams on the Reddies River and Roaring River. Both of these projects will be for flood control primarily; but, as in the case of the W. Kerr Scott Reservoir, they would produce potable water supplies and recreational areas as well. (The proposed new reservoirs will be even larger than the 1,470 maximum pool acreage of the W. Kerr Scott Reservoir. The approved Reddies River Reservoir will cover 2,056 acres at maximum pool, and the proposed Roaring River Reservoir is due to cover 2,623 acres at maximum pool.*) Other studies are being made under the direction of the North Carolina Department of Water Resources, particularly on the ground water side of the picture. And finally, the county has obtained FHA funds for a countywide engineering study that is currently underway by the firm of W. K. Dickson and Co., Inc., of Charlotte, N.C.

---

*Ibid.

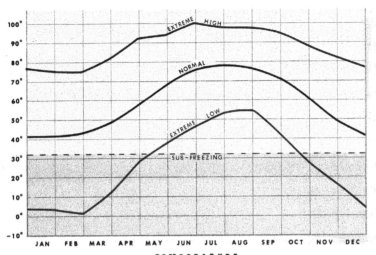

TEMPERATURE
Normal Monthly & Extremes

FIGURE 1

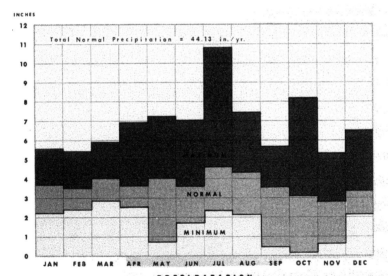

PRECIPITATION
Normal, Maximum, & Minimum Monthly

FIGURE 2

Source: U. S. Department of Commerce weather data, based on information from
Smith Reynolds Airport Winston Salem, N. C., 1931-1964.

While much more detailed information is being compiled, it suffices to say that water in Wilkes County is in good supply in most areas at the present time and efforts are being made to protect this supply for future use. More detailed information concerning water systems present will be included in the forthcoming Public Facilities Plan, as well as in the other studies mentioned above.

Climate

Wilkes County meteorological information is somewhat limited, and, the climate is considerably varied due to the wide elevation range that is present. General temperature and precipitation information can be given for the Wilkesboros and much of the Yadkin River Valley based on data from Winston-Salem, which has about the same elevation as the central portion of the county. (See Figures 1 and 2.)

In the lower elevations the temperatures are generally favorable with monthly "normal" temperatures running from near 40°F in December and January to 78°F in July. The mean annual temperature for Wilkes County is in the range of 57°F, compared with about 59°F for the State.*

One condition worthy of note regarding the slopes of the Brushy and Blue Ridge Mountains is the temperature inversion that is experienced at certain times of the year. This condition occurs when air on the higher slopes is cool, along with that of the valley floors, leaving a "thermal belt" of relatively warm air on the middle elevation slopes of some of the mountainous areas. This phenomenon is particularly important to the apple orchards on these slopes, making these areas ideal for this use when they would not otherwise be suited for fruit trees because of the frost line. Growing season is about 170 days, but may be longer in lower elevations or in the "thermal belt" areas.

*Source: A Geographical Study of Wilkes County, Division of Community Planning, 1961.

9

Area precipitation ranges are indicated by Figure 2. Again, the overall picture is favorable, but variations can be noticable due to the differences in elevation. For example, the County has had a summer drought occasionally, and some portions of the County may receive as much as three inches more in annual rainfall or other precipitation due to the presence of the mountains.

Being in the part of North Carolina with "prevailing westerly" winds, the climate and weather is at least similar to much of the rest of the state. While temperatures may run slightly lower than other portions of the state, the mountains act as a barrier to much of the winter cold air and cause some warming of the air that moves in from central Canada and across the Plains States. This barrier is also effective regarding snowfall, with the western slopes normally receiving more snow than is received on the Wilkes County side of the Blue Ridge Mountains. Most snowfall occurs when low pressure slows or reverses a front coming across the mountains, or when a low pressure storm develops over the Gulf of Mexico and moves into the Piedmont section of North Carolina, particularly if cold weather is forcing its way across the Blue Ridge at the same time. Thunderstorms are common in summer. Hurricanes that come through the state are usually "spent" by the time they reach this area.

Soils and Geology

Much of the soil information in North Carolina has been on file for several years and was written primarily for agricultural use. Wilkes County planning officials and residents in general are fortunate, however, in that soil data has just been updated here and published in a form that is useful to those considering urban, recreational, and other more intensive uses as well as general agriculture. This information is illustrated graphically by Map 3.

There are about 40 different soil types in Wilkes County, of which some 15 major types make up the greater portion. As represented in Map 3, and the data shown in Table 1, these major types have

10

GENERALIZED SOILS MAP

LEGEND

- CECIL - PACOLET
- CHESTER - ASHE - HAYESVILLE
- ASHE - CHANDLER
- SURRY
- CECIL
- CECIL - APPLING
- CONGAREE - CHEWACLA
- WICKHAM - WEBOWEE
- LOUISBURG - HIWASSEE
- STONY STEEP LAND

WILKES COUNTY
NORTH CAROLINA

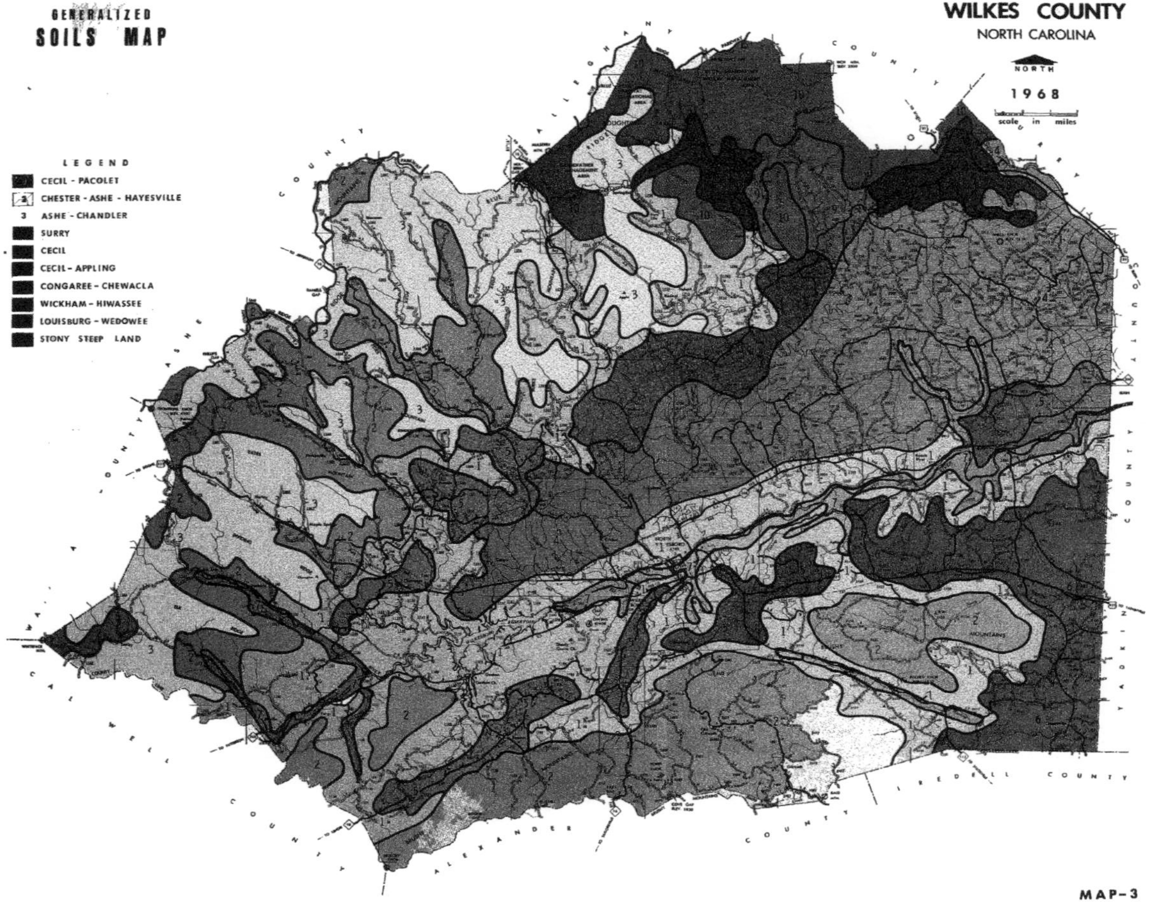

1968

NORTH

scale in miles

MAP-3

been grouped into 10 "associations" for a general overall analysis
of the soils of the county. This analysis was made by representatives of the U. S. Department of Agriculture, Soil Conservation
Service, and the information given here is naturally very general
since an attempt is made to "look" at the soils of an entire county
almost at one time. For those who need specific information for
smaller tracts of land, more detailed information is available at
the local USDA offices along with expert advice on planning and
management of individual tracts, whether for agricultural or urban
use.

Briefly, the 10 soil associations, their locations, and their
major features and limitation factors are outlined as follows:

1. Cecil-Pacolet: This association occupies about 23% of the
    county and is located in fairly narrow bands along the Yadkin
    River and at the base of the Brushy and Blue Ridge Mountains.
    It is well-drained, moderately deep, upland soils with firm,
    clay to clay loam subsoils on fairly narrow ridges and choppy
    sloping to steep side slopes. Dominant slope is from 10% to
    25%. There are moderate to severe limitations to septic tank
    use, light industry, and roads due to percolation, shrink-swell
    and traffic-supporting factors.

2. Chester-Ashe-Hayesville: This association occupies some 19%
    of the county and is located primarily in the Brushy Mountains
    and smaller areas of the smoother topography of the Blue Ridge.
    It is well and somewhat excessively drained, shallow to moder-
    ately deep, upland soils with friable, fine sandy loam to clay
    subsoils on narrow ridges and long sloping to steep side slopes.
    Dominant slope is from 20% to 40%. Development limitations
    include moderate to severe degrees for sewer systems, septic
    tanks, intensive play areas, light industry and roads. These
    limitations are largely due to such factors as steep slopes,
    rocks, and traffic-supporting capacity.

3. Ashe-Chandler: This association occupies about 16% of the
    total county area and is located in the northern and northwest
    section in the Blue Ridge Mountains. It is somewhat excessively
    drained, shallow and moderately deep, upland soils with friable
    silt loam and fine sandy loam subsoils on very narrow ridges
    and steep and very steep side slopes. Dominant slope range is
    from 35% to 50%. Development limitations are mostly severe for
    such uses as sewerage systems, septic tanks, intensive play
    areas, light industry and roads. Limitations are primarily
    due to steep slopes, rock presence, or low traffic-supporting
    capability.

11

4. Surry: This assocation involves about 15% of the county and is located in a large area through the central and eastern part of Wilkes. This is well-drained, moderately deep, micaceous, upland soils with friable silty clay to clay subsoils on fairly broad ridges and sloping to steep side slopes. The dominant slope is from 5% to 15%. There is moderate limitation to development uses for septic tanks, light industry, and roads, due to percolation rate, shrink-swell potential and traffic-supporting capacity.

5. Cecil: The fifth of the larger associations, this category occupies about 11% of the county. It is located in several areas through the central part of the county, with some of the larger areas around Mulberry, Hays, Dockery, and an area north and east of Ronda. This is well-drained, deep, upland soil with firm clay subsoils on fairly broad ridges and sloping to steep side slopes. Dominant slope is from 5% to 15%. Development problems are few with this association; however, moderate limitations are noted for septic tanks, light industry, and roads, due to percolation, possible shrink-swell, and traffic-bearing capacity.

6. Cecil-Appling: This association makes up about 6% of the county and is located in one block in the southeast corner. It is well-drained, deep, upland soils with firm, sandy clay to clay subsoils on fairly broad ridges and sloping to steep side slopes. Slopes are dominantly from 5% to 12%. This association has moderate limitations listed for septic tanks, light industry, and roads, due to some areas of poor percolation, shrink-swell problem areas, and possible insufficient traffic-supporting capability. It is probably the best soil for farming in the county.

7. Congaree-Chewacla: This occupies only about 2% of the county and is located primarily along the Yadkin River. It is nearly level, well and somewhat poorly drained flood plain soils with friable, silt loam, loam and silty clay loam subsois. Limitations for most uses other than agriculture are generally severe, due to the flood hazard and water table level.

8. Wickham-Hiwassee: This association occupies about 2% of the county also, and is located at the base of the Blue Ridge Mountains, east of Traphill and around Absher. The soil group is well-drained, deep, terrace soils with friable to firm clay loam to clay subsoils on fairly broad ridges and short rolling side slopes. The dominant slope is from 4% to 10%. Primary limitations to development in this association are slight to moderate classifications for recreation areas, light industries or roads, largely due to the shrink-swell potential, traffic-bearing capacity, and trafficability (sometimes sticky soil that makes foot traffic difficult).

9. **Louisburg-Wedowee:** This association makes up only about 1% of the county and is located around and to the west of Traphill. It is well-drained, shallow to moderately deep, upland soils with friable, sandy loam to sandy clay subsoils on fairly broad ridges and sloping to steep side slopes. The dominant slope range is from 6% to 15%. Limitation to development ranges from moderate to severe for such uses as sewerage systems, septic tanks, intense play areas, light industry, and roads. The limiting factors in all these cases is the presence of rock and steep slopes.

10. **Stony Steep Land:** This association makes up about %5 of the county and is found to the west of Stone Mountain and along the Wilkes-Alleghany County line. These are very shallow to moderately deep, stony, upland soils on steep and very steep slopes. Slopes in this association are greater than is normally practical for most uses, and this combined with the rock presence make the area generally severely limited ot unsuited to any development and of little use even in agriculture.

(Note: Soil information taken from General Soil Map, Wilkes County, N. C., U.S. Department of Agriculture, Soil Conservation Service, Raleigh, N.C., December, 1967.)

Geological information was covered in some detail in the earlier Division of Community Planning publication, A Geographical Study of Wilkes County. This study pointed out that the Blue Ridge Mountain area is largely hard, crystalline rocks that were thrust upward in the distant past into a mountain belt. The Brushy Mountains are composed chiefly of hard granite that has weathered into rounded knolls. The Yadkin River Valley in between the two mountain ranges provides the "transitional zone" mentioned earlier where the Piedmont part of North Carolina changes into the mountain section.

Minerals present but not exploited commercially are garnet, asbestos, kyanite and sillimanite (aluminum silicates), and gadolinite (an iron silicate). Granite gneisses are suitable for construction purposes. Mica, sands, and gravel are available for exploitation, as well as clay that is suitable for pottery.

The greatest factor of limitation for future growth and development of Wilkes County that the soil and geologic picture presents
is the ruggedness of the land itself. The chart given as Table 1
indicates some areas that are not suitable, due to soil composition,
for agricultural use, but largely the steepness of the land or rock
presence are the major limiting factors for most potential uses.

Soil Interpretations
General Soil Map
Wilkes County, N. C.

Soil Associations	Soil	% in Assoc.	LIMITATIONS FOR							Suitability for	
			Dwellings with		Recreation			Light Industries 1/	Roads and Streets 2/	General Agriculture	Woods
			Sewerage Systems	Septic Tank Filter Fields	Camp Sites	Picnic Areas	Intensive Play Areas				
1. CECIL-PACOLET (23% of county)	Cecil	40	Slight	Mod. (Perc.)	Slight	Slight	Slight	Mod. (Sh-Sw)	Mod. (TSC)	Good	Good
	Pacolet	35	Slight	Mod. (Perc. R)	Slight	Slight	Mod. (R)	Mod. (Sh-Sw)	Mod. (TSC)	Fair	Good to Fair
2. CHESTER-ASHE-HAYESVILLE (19% of county)	Chester	35	Slight	Mod. (R)	Slight	Slight	Slight	Mod. (Sh-Sw)	Mod. (TSC)	Good to Fair	Good
	Ashe	30	Mod. (R)	Sev. (R)			Sev. (R)	Mod. (R)	Mod. (R)	Poor to Fair	Good to Fair
	Hayesville	15	Slight	Mod. (R)			slight	Mod. (Sh-Sw)	Mod. (TSC)	Good to Fair	Good
3. ASHE-CHANDLER (16% of county)	Ashe	50	Mod. (R)	Sev. (R)	Slight	Slight	Sev. (R)	Mod. (R)	Mod. (R)	Poor	Good to Fair
	Chandler	20							Mod. (TSC)		Fair
4. SURRY (15% of county)	Surry	75	Slight	Mod. (Perc)	Slight	Slight	Slight	Mod. (Sh-Sw)	Mod. (TSC)	Good	Good
5. CECIL (11% of county)	Cecil	75	Slight	Mod. (Perc)	Slight	Slight	Slight	Mod. (Sh-Sw)	Mod. (TSC)	Good	Good
6. CECIL-APPLING (6% of county)	Cecil	50	Slight	Mod. (Perc)	Slight	Slight	Slight	Mod. (Sh-Sw)	Mod. (TSC)	Good	Good
	Appling	20	Slight	Mod. (Perc)	Slight	Slight	Slight	Mod. (Sh-Sw)	Mod. (TSC)	Good	Good
7. CONGAREE-CHEWACLA (2% of county)	Congaree	40	Sev. (Fl)	Sev. (Fl)	Sev. (Fl)	Mod. (Fl)	Sev. (Fl)	Sev. (Fl)	Sev. (Fl)	Good	Good
	Chewacla	25	Sev. (Fl,Wt)	Sev. (Fl,Wt)	Sev. (Fl,Wt)	Sev. (Fl,Wt)	Sev. (Fl,Wt)	Sev. (Fl,Wt)	Sev. (Fl,Wt,TSC)	Fair	Good
8. WICKHAM-HIWASSEE (2% of county)	Wickham	45	Slight	Slight	Slight	Slight	Slight	Mod. (Sh-Sw)	Mod. (TSC)	Good	Good
	Hiwassee	20	Slight	Slight	Mod. (Traf)	Mod. (Traf)	Mod. (Traf)	Mod. (Sh-Sw)	Sev. (TSC)	Good	Good
9. LOUISBURG-WEDOWEE (1% of county)	Louisburg	45	Mod. (R)	Sev. (R)	Slight	Slight	Sev. (R)	Mod. (R)	Mod. (R)	Good to Fair	Good to Fair
	Wedowee	30	Slight	Mod. (R)	Slight	Slight	Mod. (R)	Mod. (R)	Mod. (R)	Good to Fair	Good to Fair
10. STONY STEEP LAND (5% of county)			Sev. (R)	Sev. (R)	Sev. (R)	Sev. (R)	Sev. (R)	Sev. (R)	Sev. (R)	Unsuited	Poor

Slopes > 10% impose limitations; 10-25% - Mod.; 25%+ - Sev. (Sewerage Systems)

Slopes > 10% impose limitations; 15% - Mod.; 15%+ - Sev. (Septic Tank Filter Fields)

Slopes > 6% impose limitations; 6-10% - Mod.; 10%+ - Sev. (Camp Sites)

Slopes > 10% impose limitations; 25% - Mod.; 25%+ - Sev. (Picnic Areas)

Slopes > 6% impose limitations; 6-10% - Mod.; 10%+ - Sev. (Intensive Play Areas)

Slopes > 10% impose sev. limitations (Light Industries)

Slopes > 25% impose sev. limitations (Roads and Streets)

Abbreviations for Limiting Factors:

Fl - Flood hazard
Wt - Water Table
Traf - Trafficability
Sh-Sw - Shrink-swell potential
R - Rock
Perc - Percolation rate
Cor - Corrosion potential
TSC - Traffic supporting capacity
Prod - Productivity
AWC - Available water capacity

Abbreviations for degree of limitations:

Slt - Slight
Mod - Moderate
Sev - Severe

1/ Structures whose footings are in subsoil.

2/ Refer to roads and streets that have subsoil for base.

U. S. DEPARTMENT OF AGRICULTURE, SOIL CONSERVATION SERVICE, RALEIGH, NORTH CAROLINA

TABLE - 1

Forestry and Wildlife

Estimates of forest land in Wilkes County vary slightly, but
the range generally agreed upon is that some 75% of the total
county area is in commercial forests or woodland from which timber
is cut and sold. Overall land area in woods or forests, including
the Blue Ridge Parkway and wildlife refuge areas, is estimated to
be as high as 82% of the county area. Translated into acreage,
this gives Wilkes some 365,000 acres of commercial forests compared to its total area of roughly 490,000 acres.

Most of the forest acreage is in the Blue Ridge and Brushy
Mountains. As the earlier soils map indicates, this land involves
good soil with fairly steep slopes, making it good for forest use
while it might not be good for numerous other uses.

Primary owners of the forest lands are individuals with small
tracts of 25 to 75 acres. Ownership and estimated 1967 acreages
and percentages are as follows:*

Owner	Acres	Per Cent of Total
Individuals	294,000	80.5
Furniture & Lumber companies	62,000	17.0
Public**	9,000	2.5
Total	365,000	100.0

The commercial forests are about 50% hardwoods and 50% pine and
soft hardwoods (such as Yellow Poplar). More specific types of
trees within these two general categories are White Pine, Shortleaf
Pine, Virginia Pine, Yellow Poplar, and miscellaneous hardwoods
(largely of the oak and hickory varities). Recent years have seen

---

*Source: Mr. Edwin McGee, Wilkes County Forester, Wilkesboro, N.C.
**Public land in this case includes Federally-owned Blue Ridge Park-
way area within the county, and the State-owned Thurmond Chatham
Wildlife Management Area.

the introduction of growing Christmas trees commercially. Since a period of 5 to 6 years is needed to reach a good yearly harvest level, this effort has not reached very high levels as yet. As of late 1967 there were some 8 to 10 growers with an estimated 35-40,000 trees. Local growers have a definite advantage in quality over trees that must be cut and shipped into the southern states from some distant point, and a good market can probably be built as production volume increases.

A wood processing industry is due to go into operation in the county within the next 18 months.* This firm is reported to require 35,000 cords of hardwood pulpwood annually once it is open, which should assist in reducing the cull hardwood present as well as adding to the local income.

Most of the timber cut in Wilkes County is used as lumber for construction of homes and other buildings. The furniture industry is a large volume user also, and some trees are now used for pulpwood. Recent volumes are estimated at about 19 million board feet being cut per year, compared with a yearly growth rate of about 15 million board feet. Forestry officials do not consider this difference alarming, however, since the total growing stock is estimated at some 50 million board feet, and the forests are apparently not being converted to other uses.

Income from the small landowner forests alone is estimated at about $500,000 per year.** This amounts to about $1.70 per acre for the small forest owner. Forestry representatives feel that there is a potential for increased income here, provided there is proper management, care, and marketing by landowners. (The maximum income to be expected with proper management is given at $20 per acre.)

*Source: The Journal Patriot, North Wilkesboro, N.C., July 1, 1968.
**Source: Mr. Edwin McGee, Wilkes County Forester, Wilkesboro, N.C.

Other forestry problems in the county, in addition to forest management, include fire control, a large amount of cull hardwood trees that should be cut out and replaced by better types, and a labor shortage of workers needed to put the better forestry practices of culling and replanting into effect. (The State, for example, will arrange to have forests culled and replanted at a reasonable fee of landowners which many are willing to pay, but difficulty is experienced in obtaining workers to do this work even at a reasonable hourly wage.)

Wildlife and its recreational potential is closely related to forestry in that the preservation and conservation of forests also provides cover for wildlife and preserves this feature of nature. While hunting and fishing has not been exploited in the immediate past except by local residents, it appears that there is some potential for the promotion of these sports. There were sufficient quantities of bear and deer to allow a limited hunting season in 1967-68, and small game available included rabbits, squirrels, quail, foxes, raccoons, and opossums. Fish available for sport includes Mountain Trout in designated streams in addition to the normal warm water fishes. The W. Kerr Scott Reservoir offers bass, bream and cat-fishing.

Information on forestry management, seedling supplies and other assistance along these lines can be obtained through the offices of the Wilkes County Forester in Wilkesboro.

FOLDOUT

part 2

FOLDOUT

PART II

LAND POTENTIAL STUDY

LAND USE SURVEY AND ANALYSIS

To plan for the future use of land, it is important to consider its present use. This was done in Wilkes County in late
1967 by means of a countywide "windshield survey" of existing
land uses. (See Map 4) A more detailed look into this data
will follow under the topics of: (1) Existing Land Use Categories and Quantities, (2) Land Use Patterns, (3) Land Use Problems,
(4) Housing Conditions, (5) The Major Road System, and (6)
Future Land Use Projections.

EXISTING LAND USE CATEGORIES AND QUANTITIES

Since so large an area as the 765 square miles of Wilkes
County would require extensive data for detailed land use measures,
only major uses were compiled for this generalized study. The
table lists these general categories which were compiled from
U.S. Department of Agriculture soil survey estimates.

Existing Land Use Quantities (1967)

Use	Area (Sq. Miles)	Per Cent of County
Forest or woods	589	77.0
Pasture or hay	70	9.2
Row crops	66	8.6
Urban (including roads)	40	5.2
Total	765	100.0

19

FOREST OR WOODS. This category includes the 575 square miles
    that are in commercial forests, plus land that is wooded
    but not commercially harvested -- such as the land along
    the Blue Ridge Parkway and land within wildlife refuge
    areas. This is by far the largest land use in the county
    and will probably remain so due to the rugged terrain of
    much of the undeveloped land. Forest areas in the county
    are largely along the Blue Ridge and Brushy Mountain
    ranges.

PASTURE OR HAY. This is the second largest category and in-
    cludes grazing land and land that is tended for the hay
    that can be harvested yearly. This use is particularly
    encouraged by the waste material available for pasture
    fertilizer from the county's many poultry farms. The hay
    acreage remained about the same from 1960 to 1966, while
    many other crops declined in acreage during this period.
    Beef cattle numbers have increased as pasture land acre-
    age was increased. The green pastures have also made a
    marked difference in the appearance of the countryside in
    the past six to eight years.

ROW CROPS. This category includes some land that may be idle
    while in rotation with other crops and land that is in the
    "soil bank". (The 1966 reported crop acreage including
    hay amounted to about 27,500 acres or some 65 per cent of
    the 66 square miles listed under this use.) Overall crop
    land is decreasing, as shown by the 1960 and 1966 reported
    crop acreages.*

URBAN. This is the most intensive use of land and is the least
    in acreage of the generalized categories. Included in this
    group are roads, residential areas, commercial (stores,
    garages, service stations, etc.), public-semi-public
    (churches, schools, sports arenas, etc.), and industrial
    uses. Roads and residences make up the largest portion
    of this category. Commercial use in the county outside
    of the Wilkesboros is largely of the neighborhood grocery
    store-service station type. Industrial use is also limited
    in this outside area. Further analysis of this urban cate-
    gory will be given later under the section on Future Land
    Use Projections.

---

*Source: Mr. Dwight Williamson, Wilkes County Agriculture
          Extension Service, Wilkesboro, North Carolina.
          The 1960 acreages (including hay) totalled 35,036
          acres compared to the 27,500 total reported in 1966.
          Hay acreage amounted to 15,000 acres in both years
          and was the largest single crop reported.

LAND USE PATTERNS

A "bird's-eye" view of the late 1967 land use in Wilkes
County is presented on Map 4. The colored areas give a general
picture of how residential, commercial (retail, service and
other types of general business including small rural stores),
industrial and resource production (the latter including rock
crushing operations, apple processing sheds, etc.), and public,
semi-public (recreation areas, race tracks, churches, etc.)
uses are distributed across the countryside. The uncolored area
represents agricultural and wooded areas and land that is left
idle.

The mountainous areas have naturally retarded or hindered
development, while smoother terrain and better soils have encouraged more intensive use of other areas. For example, the
four major classifications of urban-type uses listed above are
more intensified near the Wilkesboros in the Fairplains,
Mulberry, Millers Creek, Cricket, Moravian Falls, and Oakwoods
communities. The more dense development has also gravitated to
the major highways in the east (NC 268 and US 421) and into the
communities of Hays and West Elkin. In the latter two cases,
favorable farming soils and the availability of employment in
Elkin just across the county line have been important factors
toward development. Ronda (the only incorporated town in the
county except for the Wilkesboros, population 510 in 1960),
Roaring River, and Traphill are historic settlement areas, but
there has been no sizable population growth in these communities.

The railroad stretching into the county from the east has
not fostered development except at its western end where North
Wilkesboro was born. The topography of the land has caused
this, as the railroad follows the narrow Yadkin River bed and
is somewhat cut off from higher ground by steep slopes and
rocky ledges.

Strip development, scattered commercial land use mixed with residential use, is quite pronounced along some roadways. This is particularly true of NC 16 from the Wilkesboros through Cricket and Millers Creek, along NC 268 east of North Wilkesboro, and along NC 18 north of North Wilkesboro. While not yet as bad, this type of strip development is taking place along much of US 421 as well. Some highway-oriented business is both necessary and desirable in our present automobile age. If allowed to grow unrestrained and with no set pattern, however, this type of development can be damaging to both the residential and commercial property values concerned, may be hazardous to the main traffic arteries due to congestion at exits and entrances, and can result in unhealthy conditions where residences are faced with noise, bright sign lights, or other undesirable conditions. Strip development also generally presents a very unsightly route for travelers through the area.

In summary, the land use patterns of Wilkes County present an agreeable picture to the passerby in many sections, particularly with the backdrop of tree-covered mountains, rolling green pastures, and prosperous community scenes. There are, however, several factors that mar this picture. These factors will be discussed at some length in the following section.

LAND USE PROBLEMS

Structural Conditions

Many buildings in the county have lost their usefulness for an intended purpose and are now run down and often unused. In many cases stores, garages, houses, schools, and churches have been abandoned or replaced and left standing. Often a new building goes immediately beside an abandoned building which remains unsightly and hazardous -- particularly to children who might venture into the sagging and decaying structure. Several stores or other roadside structures have been converted into

22

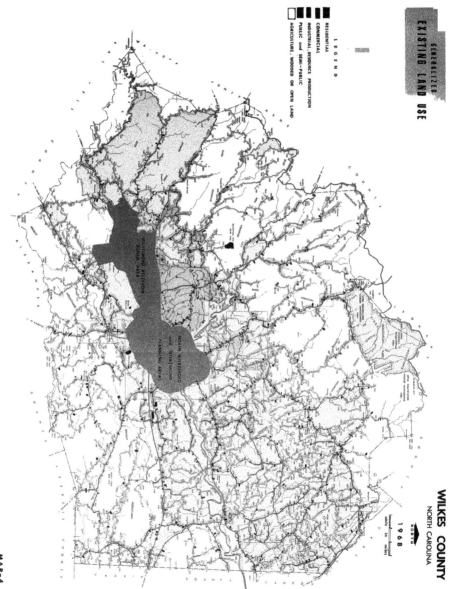

GENERALIZED
EXISTING LAND USE

L E G E N D

RESIDENTIAL
COMMERCIAL
INDUSTRIAL, RESOURCE PRODUCTION
PUBLIC and SEMI-PUBLIC
AGRICULTURE, WOODED OR OPEN LAND

WILKESBORO RESERVOIR
ZONING AREA

NORTH WILKESBORO
and WILKESBORO
PLANNING AREAS

WILKES COUNTY
NORTH CAROLINA

NORTH

1968

scale in miles

MAP-4

residential dwellings, resulting in additions to the existing
stock of substandard homes. Such rundown buildings tend to
have far-reaching effect on a community along with the health
and safety hazard suggested. They also offer much less attractive entranceways into the county where they are found on such
major roads as US 421, NC 16 and NC 18 -- these being highways
that are frequented by interstate travelers and mountain tourists.
Often a blighting effect on the entire community may result,
and eventually the tax base or even the economic structure of
the whole surrounding area can be affected.

Junk and Refuse Dumps

Junk, garbage, and other refuse litter areas are found in
many parts of the county. The junk is not a junkyard as such,
but one or two old, discarded automobiles that have been left
by the roadside or in many cases adjacent to an otherwise neat-
appearing residence. Garbage and other refuse (cans, bottles,
boxes, etc.) are found in many small unauthorized dumps -- such
as one noted near an entrance to the W. Kerr Scott Reservoir and
along NC 16 just south of the Blue Ridge Parkway. The health
hazard here is obvious, as these dumps provide breeding places
for rats and flies. Other possible factors resulting from dumps
may be the pollution of nearby water, a generally bad impression
on the visitor, and lowered property values.

Scattered Land Use

Many land uses outside the Wilkesboros and their one-mile
perimeter area are scattered along the roads in mixed fashion.
(This is also true of the land uses within the planning area of
the Wilkesboros, but this has been covered in earlier reports
concerned only with those areas.) Residences, for example, are
often very close to such other uses as garages, stores, or in
some cases industrial operations such as lumber yards or similar

incompatible uses. While not all of this mixed, scattered land usage is necessarily bad, there are undesirable consequences which are likely to occur. Among these are:

1. Costs to rural homeowners may approach those of the urban homeowner with few of the services available to closer-in, more compact development. These costs include well and pump, septic tank, travel expenses to work or trade areas, garbage collection fees (or no service at all), and higher insurance rates where fire and police protection are not as adequate as in municipalities.

2. Public (town, county, state, or school district) expenses are increased because of scattered land use. Roads, water and sewer, and other services can be much more economical per unit served when development is compact.

3. Rural roads become hazardous where mixed land uses are crowded into a small area with improper driveway or entrance provisions.

4. The attractive appearance of the countryside is being destroyed in some areas where buildings are crowded almost onto the right-of-way, closing off an otherwise attractive view from the road.

5. Mixed land uses often result in lowered building standards, particularly in the case of a shack or poor quality garage or other business structure being located next door to good quality residential structures.

6. Overall lower quality development often results from scattered and disorderly development in the past. This often occurs in subdivisions where lots and streets are poorly laid out and designed.

Substandard Streets and Roads

There are some examples of poorly designed subdivision streets in Wilkes County. County subdivision regulations were enacted in 1951, and while this has been helpful it is not a cure-all. Some areas still have excessively long cul-de-sacs or deadend streets, and street conditions are poor in a few cases where these residential roads may have been properly constructed but have not been properly maintained. Rural roads are fairly well kept considering the terrain and other problems of a mountainous area, but there are some problems there. For example, there are several rural paved roads that are not wide enough for two cars to pass on the paved portion. Some older roads appear to have been built around barns or other buildings with hazardous curves as a result.

Some rural dirt roads in the mountain areas are in poor condition and become almost impassable in rainy weather. Much is being done by the State Highway Commission toward improvement of these rural roads, but several areas are poorly served and currently do not have the traffic to warrant more than routine maintenance.

Aesthetics

Attractive homes, commercial centers, places of work, recreation areas, and a pleasant-appearing countryside are appreciated by most people. If the county is to be attractive to new industry and business, to tourists, and to new residents there are places which need improvement from the standpoint of aesthetics. Several examples of this problem have been mentioned -- such as building conditions, junk and garbage, and mixed land uses. Other factors include road signs (most of which have been defaced by the bullets of would-be hunters or target shooters), unsightly advertising signs, poor housekeeping by business people and individual homeowners around their premises, and

25

poorly maintained roads. Much of ths unattractiveness will
require organized programs and legal means such as ordinances
and enforcement to change the present situation. A good portion of it, however, chould be changed by a concerted effort
toward a countywide "clean up, fix up" campaign by responsible
civic groups and other concerned citizens.

Housing Conditions

The Population and Economy Report for Wilkes County compared the 1960 census data for housing conditions in Wilkes
County, North Carolina, with data for the United States as
follows:

Area	Per Cent of Substandard Units*
Wilkes County	53.5
North Carolina	36.5
United States	18.2

*Substandard in this case includes all dilapidated
units and all other units lacking a full complement
of plumbing facilities.

In late 1967, when the existing land use survey was made,
(Map 4), the residential units in the county were classified as
standard, deteriorating or dilapidated. Criteria for classify-
ing a unit were:

Standard. Unit in generally good repair except for such
minor items as need of repainting, and yard area maintenance
(at least minor landscaping).

Deteriorating. Unit appears to need more than routine maintenance. Examples of this would be rotting window frames,
porch, or other parts of the exterior; broken windows, roof,
or weatherboarding with broken or missing pieces, cracks in
the foundation, loose or missing bricks on the exterior of
the unit. Yard may indicate less interest, with some litter
or junk.

Dilapidated. The unit is obviously in poor condition, in
need of complete rebuilding or replacement. Major items
such as foundation, walls, or roof are broken or sagging;
extensive fire or storm damage is evident. Yard and premises
show little pride of ownership, are cluttered or not maintained.

26

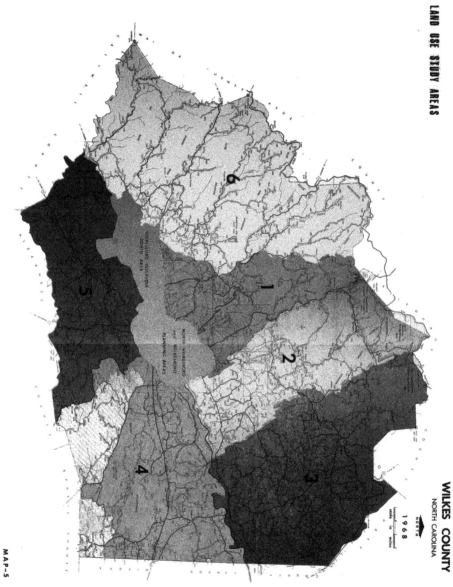

LAND USE STUDY AREAS

WILKES COUNTY
NORTH CAROLINA

1968

NORTH

scale in miles

MAP-5

To facilitate the handling of data in the house count and classification survey, the county was divided into six study areas. The Wilkesboros and their one-mile perimeters and the zoned area around the W. Kerr Scott Reservoir were not included in these six study areas because previous planning publications have covered them. The study areas were delineated by certain natural boundaries (rivers, roads, ridgelines, etc.) and were related as much as possible by community similarity. Township boundaries are also considered, and groups of townships were delineated into study areas as nearly as practicable. These study areas are illustrated by Map 5.

Based on the above methodology, the following data was computed for the six study areas.

TABLE 2 WILKES COUNTY DWELLING UNIT COUNT AND CONDITION, November, 1967

Study Area	Total Dwell. Units	Per Cent	Standard Dwell. Units	Per Cent	Deteriorating Dwell. Units	Per Cent	Dilapidated Dwell. Units	Per Cent	Mobile Homes
1	2,002	100.0	1,295	64.6	573	28.7	134	6.7	136
2	1,298	100.0	631	48.6	579	44.6	88	6.8	88
3	2,435	100.0	1,262	51.8	907	37.3	266	10.9	156
4	1,493	100.0	629	42.0	628	42.2	236	15.8	97
5	919	100.0	500	54.5	291	31.7	128	13.8	53
6	1,144	100.0	347	30.4	572	50.1	225	19.5	64
Total	9,291	100.0	4,664	50.1	3,550	38.3	1,077	11.6	594

NOTE: Due to the "temporary" nature of mobile homes, these dwelling units were enumerated separately and are not reflected in the Total Dwelling Unit figures. Further discussion will follow on the mobile homes in the county.

Source: Division of Community Planning

The highest percentage of dilapidated homes is in the more mountainous study areas numbered 4, 5, and 6. This is understandable, since more homes have been built in recent years in the closer-in study areas 1, 2 and 3. This factor makes the percentage of dilapidated homes, therefore, higher in the areas where fewer homes are located. It was interesting to note, however, that in the course of making the survey there was no particular "pattern" of dilapidated homes, and that this type of structure was found scattered throughout the county.

Another look at housing conditions can be obtained by considering the total substandard units -- the term in this case includes both the deteriorating and the dilapidated units. Substandard housing, as defined for Study Areas 1 through 5, amounted to 35.4, 51.4, 48.2, 58.0, 45.5, and 69.9 per cent, respectively. Area 1 was significantly low, again since it contains the Millers Creek, Mulberry, and Fairplains communities where many newer homes are located. At the other end of the scale is Area 5 which contains much of the sparsely settled Blue Ridge Mountain section, and Area 4 which includes a good portion of the Brushy Mountains. The overall average was computed at 49.8 per cent for substandard housing in all the study areas combined.

Mobile homes are apparently serving a growing housing need in the county. They now make up about 5.5 per cent of all the houses counted, a figure which held true in almost every study area. By the same token, there is almost no duplex or multi-family housing available outside the Wilkesboros -- a factor which no doubt encourages the use of mobile homes. Young couples and retired couples are usually interested in housing that does not require a large initial investment, and the mobile home with its pre-furnished feature is largely filling this need. Most of these units are on separate lots near a single-family dwelling. The few mobile home parks that are available are fairly small. This type of dwelling unit should be considered carefully in future planning and zoning due to its common use at the present, and due to the fact that mobile home units can quickly cause problems (i.e., lot space, and sewer facilities) when their use is not regulated properly.

Mobile home parks are encouraged when they are designed to include privacy for individual spaces, adequate water and sewer facilities, central recreation areas, and other attractive features. The use of proper design can provide healthy and desirable surroundings.

The Major Road System

Wilkes County's major road system includes two U. S. Highways and four N. C. Highways in addition to the other paved and non-paved road mileages.

US 421 crosses the lower half of the county in an east-west direction, and US 21 cuts across the northeast corner in a southeast-northwest direction (Map 6). NC 268 also crosses the lower half of the county in a generally northeast to southwest alignment. NC 15 and NC 18 pass through the western half of the county roughly north-south semi-circles that intersect in the Wilkesboros. NC 115 serves the southeastern corner of the county, running southeast to northwest.

As of January, 1968, the North Carolina State Highway Commission office at North Wilkesboro reported a total of almost 1,238 miles of roads for which they are responsible in Wilkes County.

Primary roads (all paved)	138.5 miles
Secondary (paved)	315.0 miles
Secondary (unpaved)	784.3 miles
	1,237.8 miles

Not all of the county's roads and streets are included in these figures. Not included, for example, are municipal streets in the Wilkesboros that are not state-maintained. Any subdivision or rural roads that are not on the state system woule likewise not be included in these figures.

Map 6 gives the 1966 average daily traffic counts for
several points in the county. Traffic runs heavier in the half
of the county from the Wilkesboros east due to the mountain barrier in the west. US 421 carried an average of 2,400 vehicles
as it entered eastern Wilkes County, reached a high of 8,150
vehicles near North Wilkesboro, and carried a 1,600 vehicle
average near the western edge of the county.

NC 268 had a 4,800 vehicle per day average near West Elkin
at the county's eastern boundary and an 8,800 vehicle count just
east of North Wilkesboro. The western end of NC 268 had an average daily count of only 420 vehicles near the Wilkes-Caldwell
County line.

NC 16 had counts of 1,450 vehicles near the southern boundary of Wilkes, 4,100 in Moravian Falls, 4,400 in Cricket, and 900
at the Wilkes-Ashe County line on the west. NC 18 was comparable
to NC 16 with 1,150 vehicles at the southern boundary and a 450
count in the north at the Wilkes-Alleghany County line. NC 18
and NC 268 carried the highest count reported near their junction
in eastern North Wilkesboro where 11,000 vehicles were counted.

US 21 had counts of 3,600 where it entered eastern Wilkes
and 1,100 vehicles as it exited into the mountains at the north-
eastern corner of the county. In the southeastern corner, NC 115
carried 2,000 vehicles near Wilkesboro and 1,060 at the Wilkes-
Iredell County line.

Many areas of the county are accessible by means of this
major road system, but as the amount of unpaved roads and some
of the lower traffic counts indicate, there are areas that are
not as readily accessible as others. In addition, the more
mountainous areas have some large sections that still have few
if any roads due to the sparse population to be served and the
rough terrain there.

Traffic through these areas is restricted and future development will be hindered until more and better roads are available.
Snow and ice conditions also effect much of this same area. Even

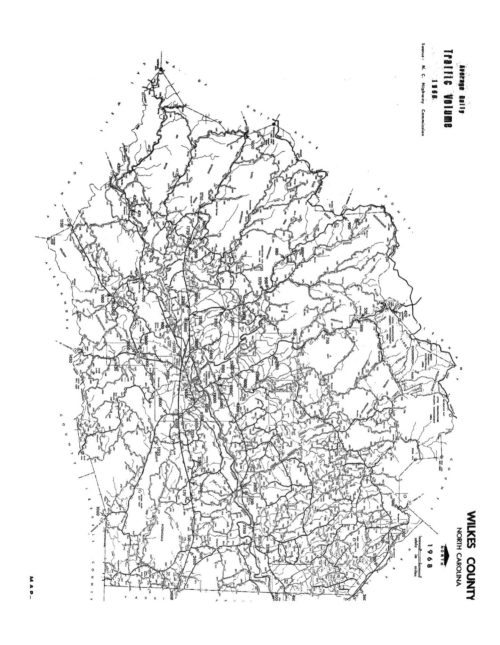

WILKES COUNTY
NORTH CAROLINA

1968

NORTH

scale in miles

though snow is cleared from the roadbed fairly quickly, ice spots continue to be hazardous as the snow melts and refreezes during cold nights. Melting snow also seeps into the supporting road-bed, weakening the support of the soil underneath and causing broken pavement.

Progress is being made in the overall road system, with several roads recently realigned and paved, and others are being improved. NC 16 south was improved in 1967, and the US 421 By-pass south of the Wilkesboros is nearing completion. Other por-tions of US 421 were upgraded within recent years. Due to the terrain and the construction practices of earlier days, however, much of the primary and secondary road system in the county is now "outdated" for today's traffic speeds and will become more inadequate during the planning period to 1990. Major roads and streets will require much planning and expense in the future if the county is to keep pace with other portions of the state and nation.

FUTURE LAND USE PROJECTIONS

An important consideration in planning for future land use needs is the relation of the present land use to the present pop-ulation. This present relationship can then shed light on how much land should be planned for a given population projection, along with local and national standards concerning the ideal ratio of land to people for the various uses.

The present urban land use (including roads) amounts to about 40 square miles, or 25,600 acres of Wilkes County land. Primary consideration will be given to this category in the future land use projections since the other general categories (forests, pasture, and crop lands) are less subject to change with growth except to be taken up by more intensive uses such as residential, industrial, etc. The projected urban category will then be rel-lated to the other general categories in the final analysis of this section.

31

The existing urban land breakdown is shown in the following table. Also included are the "acres per 100 persons" for each use from which factors were determined to apply to projected future population, along with other assumptions or adjustment factors, to determine the land needed for each use by 1990 in the county (exclusive of Wilkesboro and North Wilkesboro).

TABLE 3

WILKES COUNTY, EXISTING LAND USE QUANTITIES AND PROJECTED NEEDS (Urban-type uses only)

Use	Existing Acreage[1]	Acreage per 100 Persons[2]	Factor Used for Projection[3]	Additional Acreage Needed by 1990[4]
Residential	10,200	20.5	2.0	3,100
Commercial	400	.8	1.5	92
Industrial	595	1.2	10.0	900
Public-Semi-Public (excluding Blue Ridge Parkway land)	1,500	3.0	5.0	1,140
Roads and Streets	12,905	25.5	1.5	2,900
Total	25,600	51.0	--	8,132

[1] Estimates based on USDA Soil Survey, Division of Community Planning "windshield" survey of late 1967, and data from prior Wilkesboro and North Wilkesboro studies by Division of Community Planning.

[2] Based on Division of Community Planning estimate of 1967 population of 50,530.

[3] Factors were determined by relating present land use to anticipated future use, based on trends and growth prospects listed in the text.

[4] Based on factors mentioned above and projected 1990 population of 58,150. Example: (Residential use) 58,150 (1990)
$$\frac{-50,530 \ (1967)}{7,620 \ \text{Pop. Increase}}$$

Thus, 76.2 (100 persons) x 20.5 x 2.0 = 3,100 additional acres needed.

Source: Division of Community Planning

Other assumptions used in determining the future land projection factors included the following:

1. That the county will experience growth in population at or
   near the projected population figures used;

2. That there will be a continuation of the trend toward larger
   residential lots with large lawns and parking areas for
   personal cars;

3. That the trend of growth will continue to spread away from
   the older parts of the towns toward their fringe areas.
   This could increase development around the Wilkesboros, and
   will continue to be a factor since persons who work in
   places as far away as Winston-Salem, Hickory or Statesville
   but prefer a semi-rural residential area will seek rural
   areas for their homes;

4. That the trend toward the "low-profile" in commercial and
   industrial structures will continue. In shopping areas,
   even single businesses are influenced by the one-story
   buildings. Industries use this idea also since they must
   provide parking for employees on a site which is sufficiently
   large to provide for landscaping, plant expansion. This
   trend is also evident in public uses such as churches,
   schools, and governmental buildings;

5. That the demand will continue to grow for more and larger
   outdoor recreation areas for camping, picnicking, and more
   active sports;

6. That the demands of transportation for individuals will
   continue to grow, requiring wider and safer roadways to
   meet the demands of increased traffic.

In addition to these fairly general assumptions, other
local situations were considered in computing future land needs.
For example, little industry is now present in the county outside the Wilkesboros but potential sites are available; therefore, a higher factor was used. In the case of public uses, the
park and reservoir areas already planned would indicate a higher
use factor.

The 8,132 acres projected for additional urban land use
would increase the present urban land by 12.7 square miles.
This would give a total of 52.7 square miles of the county's
765 square miles in urban use by 1990.

The projected change in this urban land should be related
to the more general categories of forests, pasture, and row
crop land (see Table under Existing Land Use Categories and
Quantities Section). Much of the projected residential acreage,
for example, would have to come from existing crop land due to
the trend toward less cultivated crops each year and the fact
that developers can subdivide open land at a lower cost than
wooded land. This tendency to use open land would also hold
true for commercial and industrial development. Roads and
recreation areas would probably take some wooded acreage, but
the topography of much of the latter would tend to minimize
its being taken up to any great extent during this period.

Translated into square miles, the general categories for
land use within the county are compared below by present estimates and those for 1990.

Use	Area in Square Miles		Per Cent of Total County Land	
	1967	1990	1967	1990
Forest or woods	589	585	77.0	76.5
Pasture or hay	70	69	9.2	9.0
Row crops	66	58	8.6	7.5
Urban (including roads)	40	53	5.2	7.0
Total	765	765	100.0	100.0

Source: DCP estimates based on 1967 countwide land use
survey, plus additional land use needs projected.

Of course, the projected population and land needs will be
subject to many variances and trends during the next 20 years.
The terrain and other natural features of the county will continue
to heavily favor the rural, predominantly wooded countryside,
however, provided no large scale misuse of the land is allowed by
its residents.

POPULATION AND ECONOMY REVIEW

The Wilkes County Population and Economy Study was published in October, 1962. Some of the main points of that study are:

-- The county has turned from a traditional agricultural base to a growing specialization in lumber, furniture, and textile manufacturing. Farm jobs decreased more than employment gains elsewhere between 1950 and 1960, but jobs for women increased by 45 per cent.

-- Employment projections indicate a seven per cent gain (about 1,000 jobs) by 1970, largely from expansion of professional and commercial services.

-- The county lagged far behind state levels of income, education, and housing in the 1960 census. Half of the families in Wilkes had incomes under $3,000 and lived in substandard housing at that time.

-- Outmigration was heavy (with most of the people leaving being young adults), and a decrease in population of about five per cent by 1980 was projected.

This earlier study was somewhat pessimistic, but it was based on the 1960 census data and other standard information available at the time. In considering some changes that have occurred in the seven years since 1960, however, it appears that sufficient data is available to warrant at least some revision in the projected population figures for Wilkes County.

Among the favorable information that tends to support a brighter outlook for Wilkes is the U.S. Department of Commerce Census of Business for 1963. This report compares the business years of 1958 and 1963. Between these years the county experienced increase of approximately 21 per cent in retail trade, 31 per cent in wholesale trade, and 39 per cent in added manufacturing value.

Recent population estimates show an increase rather than a decrease in county population, and an actual house count made in connection with the land use survey also supports this trend.* Based on these and other favorable indicators, the population projection figures used in connection with current planning efforts are noted below:

Wilkes County, 1960 Population and Projections to 1990

1960 (actual)	1970	Per Cent Increase	1980	Per Cent Increase	1990	Per Cent Increase
45,269	51,950	14.7	54,930	5.8	58,150	5.9

Source: Division of Community Planning. Projections by Arithmetic Method (numerical change) using census data for 1940, 1950 and 1960, with current Division of Community Planning estimate of 50,530 persons -- based on field survey and 3.6 persons-per-dwelling unit counted.

The greater Wilkesboros area (the towns and their respective township areas) were projected at the same rate as given above with the resulting figures of 15,375 persons by 1970; 16,270 by 1980; and 17,232 by 1990. (The comparable 1960 population for this area was 13,405.)

The above figures are considered reasonable for the Land Development Plan that follows -- although they are much more optimistic than the previous population and economy study. No one, of course, can look into the future and determine exact growth rates or numbers, but it is very evident that Wilkes is growing and should plan accordingly.

---

*1965 estimate for the county by Dr. C. Horace Hamilton and Eun Sul Lee (of N.C. State University) was 49,396 persons.

UTILITIES

The future growth and development of the county can be greatly affected by public utilities and where they are readily available. If the county is to encourage industrial and population growth it must be able to serve this growth. The utility potential is discussed in the following paragraphs.

WATER AND SEWER

There is an abundance of "raw" water. Wilkesboro is well supplied from the W. Kerr Scott Reservoir and North Wilkesboro gets its water from the Reddies River. Proposed flood control dams on the Reddies River and Roaring River will further enhance county water sources.*

There are water systems in the Millers Creek-Cricket and Mulberry-Fairplains communities, both of which are supplied from the North Wilkesboro system. Expansion to take care of the needs of these systems was proposed in the North Wilkesboro Community Facilities Plan.**

A fairly new water system has been established in the Hays community to the northeast of North Wilkesboro. Water service is also available in Moravian Falls-Oakwoods community to the south, and to West Elkin on the eastern boundary of the county.

Sewer service is not as widespread, with coverage presently limited to the Wilkesboros. The outlying communities that receive water do not receive sewer service.

---

*The U.S. Corps of Engineers, Charleston, S.C. Office indicates that the Reddies River project is authorized and will be re-studied for current feasibility in fiscal year 1969. The Roaring River Reservoir is a proposed project.
**Division of Community Planning, June, 1966.

The county is taking steps in the right direction toward improvement of these important services and a countywide engineering study is underway to consider this matter in detail. This study, along with the <u>Public Facilities Plan now in process</u>, should provide much information for future consideration in this area.

ELECTRIC POWER

The Duke Power Company supplies most of the electricity used in the county, providing coverage for all of the central portion and most of the development along the major roads leading from this core. There is some REA coverage provided in areas to the east, south, far west, and northwest. There is no REA office in Wilkes, but this power comes from cooperative organizations of neighboring Davie Electric, Blue Ridge Electric, and the Surry-Yadkin Electric cooperatives. With these operations in Wilkes, virtually any electrical demand could be met from the largest industrial demand to a connection for a vacation cottage.

TELEPHONE

The more urbanized portions of the county (the Wilkesboros and areas along nearby major highways) receive telephone service from the Central Telephone Company in North Wilkesboro. The Wilkes Telephone Membership Corporation was formed about ten years ago and since that time has been engaged in providing service to the more rural parts of the county. It currently has exchanges in the communities of Boomer, Champion, Clingman, and Lomax and has been experiencing a steady growth since its formation.

NATURAL GAS

There is presently no natural gas line into Wilkes County.
Any firms or individuals that require gas must be serviced from
bottled or bulk service outlets that are locally available.
Recent announcement of a wood processing (hardboard) industry
that is to go into operation may bring this service to the
county in the near future; however, a major natural gas company
has estimated that gas service will be available to at least the
Wilkesboros area of the county within two years.*

DEVELOPMENT POTENTIAL AREAS

This portion of the Land Potential Study is designed to
inventory and delineate in a very general way the best potential
areas for various future land use needs. Such factors as soils,
topography, and other natural features are considered along with
man-made features in order to point out the best potential usage
of the land and existing resources.

The elements of agriculture and forestry, and the urban uses
of residential, commercial, industrial and public-semi-public
land will be discussed without particular regard to the amount
of land in each category anticipated during the planning period
(1968-1990).

The Land Development Plan (Part III of this report) will
then relate the potential areas to the projected population and
other pertinent factors in allocating more specific areas in the
form of a more definite plan.

*Source: The Journal Patriot, North Wilkesboro, N.C. July 4, 1968

AGRICULTURAL AND FORESTRY POTENTIAL

This category, which includes farm land, pasture, and wooded land, comprises about 95 per cent of Wilkes County at the present. There will be some conversion of this land to more intensive uses but it is anticipated that farming (centered mostly around the large poultry industry) will continue to be important for some-time to come. Much of the forests will also remain, due to the mountainous terrain that discourages other uses plus local interest in forestry and the economic benefits which go along with it.

As shown on Map 7, the better agricultural land is largely in the central and eastern parts of the county, with some smaller pockets of land in the lower west central area. Due to the eco-nomic value of this land to the county and the simple "good sense" of agricultural conservation, it is important that this rich, tillable soil be reserved for agricultural use.

Map 7 also indicates the forestry potential areas. As in the case of farm land, the forests should be protected from excessive inroads. The areas delineated are largely the mountain-ous southern, western and northwestern parts of the county. Parts of these areas can also serve for recreational use as will be discussed in the public, semi-public section.

RESIDENTIAL POTENTIAL

Natural features are very important in selecting land for homes. For example, steep slopes and low floodplain areas must be avoided. There are many areas in the mountains, of course, that provide good sites for "weekend" homes or even scattered permanent residences, but the primary concern here is for future suburban growth of the subdivision development type which is now common.

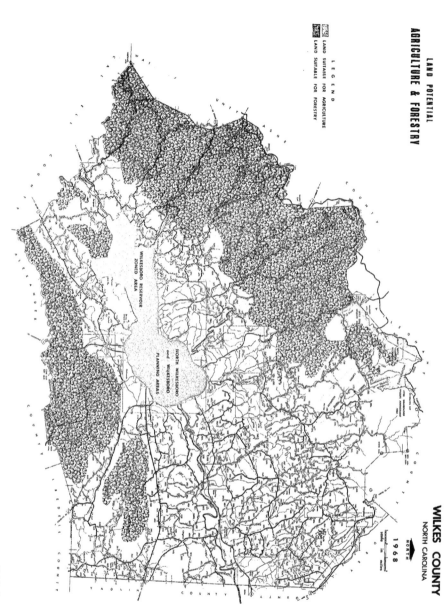

LAND POTENTIAL
AGRICULTURE & FORESTRY

LEGEND
LAND SUITABLE FOR AGRICULTURE
LAND SUITABLE FOR FORESTRY

WILKESBORO RESERVOIR
ZONED AREA

NORTH WILKESBORO
and
NORTH WILKESBORO
PLANNING AREA

WILKES COUNTY
NORTH CAROLINA

NORTH

1968

MAP-7

Map 8 approximates the land that is potentially good for
additional residential development. With some of the same requirements found in good agricultural soils, this area also falls in
the central and eastern portions of the county. Naturally, the
initial areas for growth should be those around the existing
heavily populated areas where water and some sewer facilities are
available. These initial areas for growth include land around
the Wilkesboros and the communities of Millers Creek, Cricket,
Mulberry, Fairplains, Moravian Falls, Oakwoods, Hays, and West
Elkin. Other important areas (subject to slope and septic tank
suitability of individual lots) would be along US 421 west to
the foot of the Blue Ridge Mountains, along NC 18 in the southwest, along US 421 east of North Wilkesboro, and along NC 268
both east and west from the Wilkesboros. One further good potential area would be along the paved State Road 1002 as far northeast as the Hays community and a sizable area around it.

Residential growth concentrated in these areas would have
the advantage of the better natural features, be located near
major traffic arteries for good access to the Wilkesboros or
areas outside of the county, and would make the possibility of
extending water and sewer services more feasible in the future.

Additional prime residential areas not designated on this
map include the land surrounding the W. Kerr Scott Reservoir and
that land in the vicinity of the proposed Reddies River and
Roaring River Reservoirs. The former area is already being
steadily developed, and the latter two areas are sure to encourage residential growth along with the flood control and recreational benefits that will follow with the completion of these
projects.

41

COMMERCIAL POTENTIAL

The commercial potential is quite naturally closely related to residential land use. Aside from some strictly highway-oriented businesses, the commercial centers must be near the customers or within easy access to them. Natural features should also be considered such as topography, flood hazards, and weight-bearing capability of the soil.

Much of the additional commercial development within the next few years will no doubt occur in or near the Wilkesboros, but as shown on Map 8, there are numerous outlying areas that may be utilized for commercial purposes as anticipated residential development spreads and as tourism is promoted. There is at least some form of convenience goods operation already within most of these areas, such as a neighborhood grocery store-service station, but there will be more demand for other concerns as the population and tourism increase. For example, almost limitless commercial activities are possible if the Stone Mountain Park complex does materialize as anticipated, along with the two proposed reservoirs. Coupled with the existing reservoir area and the Blue Ridge Mountain range, this commercial or commercial-recreational potential (in the form of amusement areas, motels, restaurants, etc.) could well develop into the most important economic factor in Wilkes County. This commercial development will likely gravitate toward major roads. Efforts should be made, however, to group this commercial development near intersections and other likely locations that will provide sufficient room for customers to enter, leave and park safely.

INDUSTRIAL POTENTIAL

Industry has been located almost entirely within Wilkesboro and North Wilkesboro in the past, but such factors as lack of space and the tendency toward large, spacious sites indicate that other parts of the county will become important in this growth in the future.

42

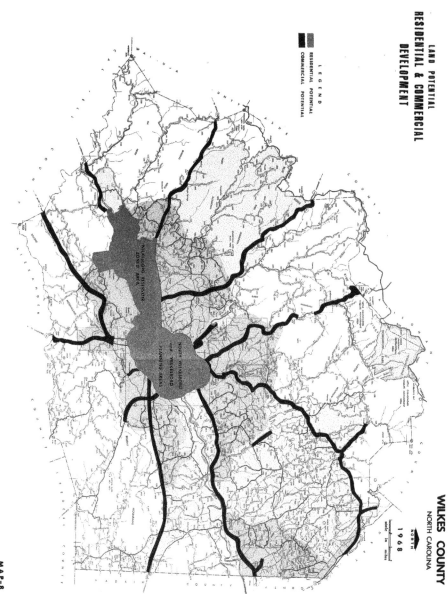

LAND POTENTIAL
RESIDENTIAL & COMMERCIAL
DEVELOPMENT

LEGEND

RESIDENTIAL POTENTIAL

COMMERCIAL POTENTIAL

WILKES COUNTY
NORTH CAROLINA

NORTH

1968

scale in miles

WILKESBORO ZONED AREA

NORTH WILKESBORO and WILKESBORO PLANNING AREA

MAP-8

Natural and man-made features are highly important in selecting industrial potential land due to the investments involved and the relationship of an industrial area to the remainder of the county. Due to the importance of industry to the county and surrounding areas as a whole this land should be selected carefully and preserved for this use, just as conservation practices are followed with other resources.

Map 9 shows the generalized locations of several potentially good industrial areas. Most of these areas embody several of the sought-after features of industrial land, and they were expecially selected for their dominant slope range and good soil qualities. Industrial sites in or near the Wilkesboros were not included on this map since they were covered in previous plans and are, for the most part, already zoned and set aside for industrial growth.

Areas which now have access to water systems or could be served easier include those near Wilkesboro on NC 115, 16 and 18 south, areas near Mulberry and on NC 16 and 18 north, the area east of North Wilkesboro on NC 268, the site near Millers Creek, and the areas near Hays and West Elkin.

Areas that would require on-site wells or water sources not now provided are those along US 421 east and west of the Wilkesboros and the outlying areas indicated near the Lomax, Austin, Traphill, Thurmond, and Clingman communities.

These areas should not be considered as the only potential sites for new industry in Wilkes County by any means, particularly when considering the grading and earthmoving equipment that is available today to prepare land for almost any use. They could be important areas, however, in planning for large industrial complexes or single industrial needs of the future.

PUBLIC, SEMI-PUBLIC POTENTIAL

As indicated on Map 9, the areas with physical potential
for this type of activity (largely recreational facilities) are
numerous. The largest area delineated ranges along the entire
northwest portion of the county. This is part of the Blue Ridge
Mountain range and already has such features as the Blue Ridge
Parkway and the park areas that accompany it (largely natural,
scenic attractions), Doughton Park (also in primitive or natural
state), and the Little Grandfather (or Thurmond Catham) Wildlife
management area (natural with limited hunting and fishing priv-
ileges). The additional land delineated along this ridgeline
could provide excellent recreation possibilities for public
(including commercial-type) activities such as picnicking, camping and other activities requiring a more or less natural setting.
More active uses could also be provided without harming the natural
beauty of the area, such as winter sports or rustic resort camps
for family or group vacations. At the eastern end of this general area is the impressive Stone Mountain, which is already in the
process of being made into a State Park.

Other areas delineated are found along the major rivers and
streams. The Yadkin River already has the W. Kerr Scott Reservoir, and could provide almost unlimited picnic and other semi-
natural areas along its banks. Other flood control projects are
under study for the Reddies River and Roaring River and these
would also provide the byproduct of more recreational facilities.
(See Appendix A and B.) The headwaters of these two waterways,
along with Fork Creek and Elk Creek in the western part of the
county, offer much hunting and fishing potential -- including
excellent sites for lodges, skeet clubs, etc.

Smaller areas delineated for parks and natural uses requiring little maintenance include portions of Warrior Creek and
Moravian Creek in the southwest, or such unique physical features
as Fitches Knob in the southwest and Wells Knob in the northeast
part of the county.

44

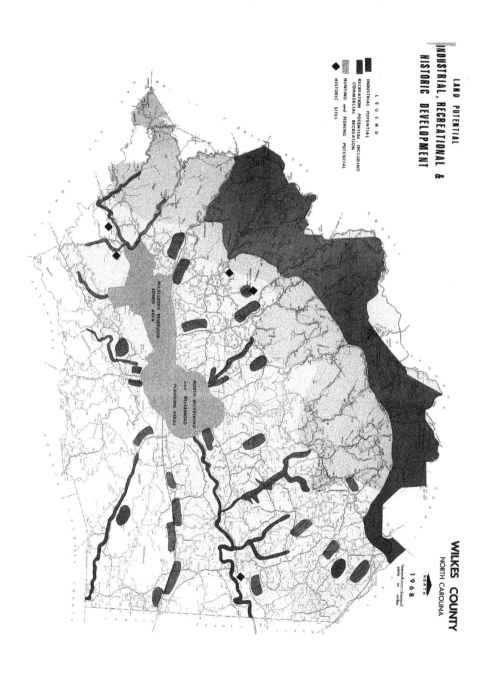

LAND POTENTIAL
INDUSTRIAL, RECREATIONAL & HISTORIC DEVELOPMENT

L E G E N D

INDUSTRIAL POTENTIAL

RECREATION POTENTIAL, INCLUDING COMMERCIAL RECREATION

RECREATION POTENTIAL, INCLUDING COMMERCIAL RECREATION

HUNTING and FISHING POTENTIAL

◆ HISTORIC SITES

WILKES COUNTY
NORTH CAROLINA

1968

NORTH

scale in miles

Finally, several possibilities for historical sites are
noted on Map 9. These include "Roundabout" -- the homeplace of
Ben Cleveland, located near Ronda; Rendezvous Mountain, a meeting
place for Cleveland and his followers, located as an undeveloped
State Park near Purlear; the log cabin of Ben Cleveland's brother
Robert, located on SR 1300 in the Parsonville community; and
Boone's cabin and Tom Dula's grave (of folklore fame) both located near Ferguson. These and other bits of history remain in
spite of minimal effort in the way of preservation in the past.
These and other sites could be important to tourism as well as
the local heritage if proper care and preservation of these
areas could be arranged and their cause promoted.

In summary, Wilkes County has much potential for growth and
development, including an excellent possibility for the promotion
of tourism to the extent that it could become possibly the major
economic factor here. If properly planned and developed, there
is no reason why Wilkes County could not help provide its citizens with additional income and related benefits from this potential and continue to be a good place to live as well.

part 3

PART III

THE LAND DEVELOPMENT PLAN

The Land Development Plan for Wilkes County has the purpose
of serving as a guide for the long-range physical development of
the county. Comprehensive in nature, the plan draws from the
development potential analysis already discussed and includes the
major factors regarding future development. This comprehensive
feature should be maintained in all future thinking and planning
by considering the county as a whole rather than as separate
townships or settlement areas.

Although necessarily general and far-reaching, the Land
Development Plan contains proposals and recommendations that are
certainly practical enough to be achieved. Any such effectuation
of the plan, however, is the joint responsibility of the governing
officials and private citizens, and support from both will be
necessary to get favorable results. Some of the tools for implementation will be discussed in Part IV of this publication.

GOALS

Before a plan is made for any undertaking, certain objectives
should be determined to give direction to the plan. What is this
comprehensive Land Development Plan for Wilkes County to accomplish?
Some of its goals are listed here:

-- Conservation and development of natural resources.
-- Development of safe and attractive residential areas.
-- Increased industrial employment and production, and
   tourism.
-- Provision for convenient business areas which are not
   scattered haphazardly along major traffic routes.

-- Encouragement of compact development which can be served
   by utilities and other services at a minimum cost to
   the public.
-- Improvement of the transportation system through and
   within the county.
-- Encouragement of the dual use of forest land -- to
   provide economic improvement and more recreational space.
-- Adoption of new and enforcement of existing planning
   tools such as zoning ordinances, subdivision regulations,
   and building and housing codes that will help implement
   the plan.

DEVELOPMENT PROPOSALS

The Wilkes County Land Development Plan is presented in
graphic form by Map 10. Details on the various elements proposed
are given in the following text. (Note: for land within Wilkesboro, North Wilkesboro, and the W. Kerr Scott Reservoir Area, see
the Future Land Use Plan, Wilkesboro, North Wilkesboro, and Wilkes
County, Division of Community Planning, December, 1962.)

RESIDENTIAL ELEMENT

Ideal residential areas are those with adequate drainage and
a slope range of 5 to 15 per cent. These areas should also be
located conveniently to places of work and schools. They should
be protected from traffic, railroads and other incompatible uses,
and should be reasonably compact in order to reduce costs for
utilities, streets, and other facilities.

As noted in the Land Use Survey and Analysis section, the
county will need some 3,100 acres to house the additional population projected for 1990. This would give a total of about
13,300 acres of residential land at that time or less than 3 per
cent of the county's total 765 square mile area.

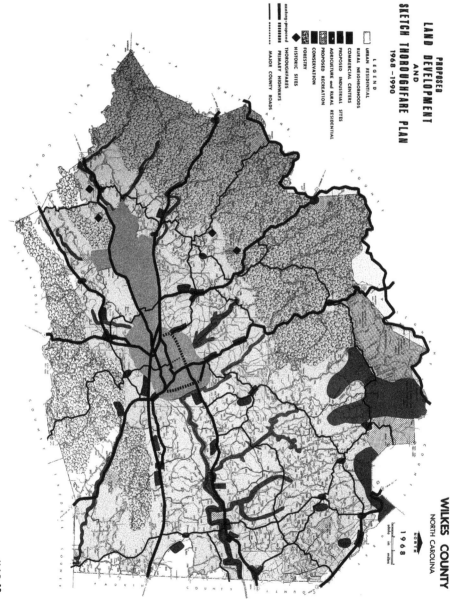

PROPOSED
LAND DEVELOPMENT
AND
SKETCH THOROUGHFARE PLAN
1968 - 1990

L E G E N D

URBAN RESIDENTIAL
RURAL NEIGHBORHOODS
COMMERCIAL CENTERS
PROPOSED INDUSTRIAL SITES
AGRICULTURE and RURAL RESIDENTIAL
PROPOSED RECREATION
CONSERVATION
FORESTRY
HISTORIC SITES
existing-proposed
THOROUGHFARES
PRIMARY HIGHWAYS
MAJOR COUNTY ROADS

WILKES COUNTY
NORTH CAROLINA

NORTH
1968

MAP-10

Future residential growth in Wilkes County should take place largely in the areas adjacent to Wilkesboro and North Wilkesboro. This central area is the focal point of the county from the transportation standpoint, and has fostered the county's economic strength since about 1900. Some growth in outlying communities can be expected as noted below.

The residential element of the plan will be discussed in the two sections which follow -- Urban Residential Areas and Rural Neighborhoods.

Urban Residential Areas

These are the proposed areas for the more intense residential development in the future. The minimum density of these areas should be no less than three dwelling units per acre or lot sizes from 8,000 square feet to 15,000 square feet. This density minimum is suggested due to the high unit cost of serving areas with streets, water and sewer, and other facilities, if a lower density is used. Of course, there are some lots now in use that are much larger than 15,000 square feet and this will continue to be true. On the other hand, the use of apartments and duplexes would keep the density average within a reasonable range.

The proposed Urban Residential Areas are (1) Wilkesboro-North Wilkesboro; (2) Hays; (3) West Elkin; and (4) Ronda. These areas are described as follows:

The Wilkesboro-North Wilkesboro Area. This includes the communities of Mulberry and Fairplains to the north, Millers Creek and Cricket to the northwest, and Moravian Falls, Oakwoods and Call to the south and east of the central Wilkesboros core. The first two settlement areas already have water systems that feed from the North Wilkesboro system. Moravian Falls and Oakwoods fall just outside of the Wilkesboro perimeter but public water is available here and attractive residential growth is taking place -- including a country club and golf course. The Call section (and Broadway, nearer to the Wilkesboros) have no water system at the present.

49

It is evident that additional urban residential growth will be attracted to this central area of Wilkesboro-North Wilkesboro due to the nearness of the trade and industrial centers. The presence of water and other services that are available, the attractive sites and good soil conditions, and the transportation system available further enhance the area. This area also includes much of the townships of Wilkesboro, Reddies River and Mulberry -- all of which were included in the townships with projected population gains in the Wilkes County Population and Economy Report.

The Hays Area. This proposed urban residential area is located on SR 1002 northeast of North Wilkesboro. Suburban homes are being built fairly rapidly along this road just outside of North Wilkesboro's one-mile perimeter, and the land use survey showed that there were many relatively new homes within the present Hays community.

The Hays community is within Rock Creek Township (which had a population of 3,094 in 1960 and was shown with a projected population gain in the Wilkes County Population and Economy Report. Other factors that would encourage residential growth here include the recently completed community water system, favorable topography and soil, good transportation connections with the Wilkesboros and NC 268 to Elkin, and potential industrial sites.

West Elkin. This area, located on the eastern county line, is an unincorporated settlement which adjoins the Town of Elkin in Surry County. Residential and commercial growth has been experienced within recent years at a much faster rate than was indicated by the 1950 and 1960 population trend. The Land Development Plan for Elkin, (Division of Community Planning, 1963), indicated only limited residential and commercial land use existing in West Elkin at that time. The comparable land use survey made for Wilkes County in late 1967 showed that considerable construction activity has taken place since the earlier survey, including residential and commercial properties and a new elementary school. It appears that this area has experienced an economic upturn just as noted earlier in this publication about the Wilkesboros.*

Due to this recent growth and favorable growth prospects for the future, it is proposed that West Elkin continue as a "bedroom" community and neighborhood shopping area for people employed in Elkin, Ronda, the Wilkesboros, and other neighboring towns. It would serve as an attractive residential area and could continue its almost "rural" atmosphere at the same time.

*Note: The U.S. Department of Commerce Census of Business shows gains in 1963 over 1958 for retail sales for Elkin at over 20%. Surry County's manufacturing value added showed an increase of almost 54%.

50

Ronda. The only incorporated town in Wilkes County except for the Wilkesboros, Ronda is proposed as a "satellite town" for the Wilkesboros. This means that Ronda would be a growing independent town and carry on its own administrative affairs, but it would be dependent on the Wilkesboros and the rest of the county for certain items such as cultural and recreational facilities. It should also coordinate its growth and plans with the remainder of the county, even though it might not be as dependent on the county as some more rural neighborhoods.

Ronda has had a major development source for many years with a sizable furniture manufacturing plant located there. It also has a garment industry that is more recent. The commercial area, while fairly old and in drastic need of improvement, has retail facilities that are not found in the more rural communities. It also has east-west (NC 268) and north-south (paved secondary) road connections and access to the railroad.

Rural Neighborhoods

Several rural neighborhoods are shown on the land development Plan (Map 10). These neighborhoods will be smaller residential concentrations with a lower development density than the urban residential areas. They include small commercial centers to provide local needs and farm supplies for the surrounding agricultural lands and to serve the motoring public.

As the county's population increases, many of these rural neighborhoods could probably support small industrial operations. Any industrial growth will necessarily be limited in most cases because of the absence of water and sewerage facilities and the lesser labor supply in these more sparsely settled areas.

Beginning in northern Wilkes and moving clockwise around the county, these rural neighborhoods delineated include the communities of McGrady, Traphill, Doughton and Thurmond, Austin, Roaring River, Clingman, Boomer, Ferguson, Champion, and Purlear. All are recognized as definite communities now although in some cases no more than a service station-grocery store and a few scattered

51

residences are located there. When related to other proposals, such as highway improvements, parks or industrial sites, all of these areas can be important elements in the overall county plan.

COMMERCIAL ELEMENT

Additional acreage projected for future commercial use was given in the Land Use Survey and Analysis as 92 acres. (Based on the earlier <u>Wilkesboro, North Wilkesboro and Wilkes County Future Land Use Plan</u> and the recent countywide survey, there are approximately 400 acres of land in commercial use at the present.) Although it is difficult to accurately scale the uses on the land development plan (Map 10), it will be noted that more land is represented than the 92 additional acres. This overage is to allow for existing commercial development plus room for expansion in areas that fit into the overall plan, to allow for a variety of sites for the projected future commercial use, and to allow for some additional areas in the event the future development should occur at a faster rate than projected.

As shown by the land development plan, the commercial areas fall largely within the urban residential and rural neighborhood residential areas described under the Residential Element of the plan. Retail, wholesale, and most service-oriented business will naturally relate to these population centers. Highway and tourist-oriented business will gravitate toward thses centers and such major highway intersections as the US 421-Bypass 421 point east of the Wilkesboros, roads that intersect near the proposed Stone Mountain Park in the northeast, and near intersections between US 421 and NC 16 and the Blue Ridge Parkway in the west.

Users of the areas indicated on the plan should be encouraged to maintain compactness to prevent such problems as traffic hazards and further mixed land use, and to use good design principles that will help to promote the health, safety and good appearance of the neighborhood where each commercial facility is located.

AGRICULTURAL AND RURAL RESIDENTIAL ELEMENT

Wilkes County continues to be an important contributor to the state and regional agricultural picture, particularly the large production of poultry in the county. For example, the number of broilers raised in the county increased from 21 million in 1960 to well over 57 million in 1966. In dollars and cents this single part of the poultry industry accounted for over $26 million in 1966.*

These figures are included to emphasize the fact that agricultural land remains important to the county in spite of the trend in recent years toward fewer farms and fewer agricultural workers. This importance of agricultural land is not likely to decrease to any great extent by 1990 and is therefore given due regard in the land development plan (Map 10).

There are now 136 square miles, or 17.8% of the total county area, in the agricultural use of pasture and row crops. Some conversion of this land is expected to meet the projected additional need for urbanization, but only some 12.7 square miles are called for if the projected requirements materialize. It is anticipated that the remaining agricultural land will follow the recent trend toward more mechanized farms and scattered residential use.

The land delineated for agricultural use follows the basic goal of preserving the better farm land for this use. Not shown in these areas, due to the map scale involved, are the numerous small commercial activities that would be desirable to serve these rural areas. These activities should be located in areas convenient to the people they serve and should have ample setback and parking space to prevent traffic hazards.

---

*Source: Mr. Dwight Williamson, Wilkes County Agricultural Extension Service, Wilkesboro. Income was based on average sale price for an average bird.

INDUSTRIAL ELEMENT

Modern industry has brought about different location requirements than was often the case in the past. Larger sites are being
required because of the horizontal layouts now common and to provide accessory areas for parking, loading and for landscaping. In
addition, the following basic location requirements are important:

-- reasonably level land, preferably with a slope range of
   5% or less;
-- well drained soil that is capable of bearing heavy
   buildings and traffic;
-- flexibility in tracts (different sizes and locations,
   minimum size of 5 acres);
-- access to transportation sytem;
-- adequate water, sewer and utilities, or reasonable
   distance from which existing facilities can be extended;
-- compatible surrounding land uses.

As computed in the land use survey and analysis section,
Wilkes County should reserve at least 900 additional acres of land
for future industrial use. The rough terrain of much of the county
makes it important that options on areas that are particularly suitable for industry be acquired through a development commission or
some other group and reserved for this purpose.

Industrial land that is within the jurisdiction of earlier
Wilkesboro and North Wilkesboro plans is not shown in the Wilkes
County Land Development Plan (Map 10). Areas that are most likely
to be put to early use are those near an existing water system.

The areas so shown include those on the US 421 Bypass near Wilkesboro, on NC 268 east near North Wilkesboro, on NC 16 near Millers
Creek, and the areas near Hays, Roaring River, and Ronda.

Areas that would require on-site wells or some special water source include those on NC 18 southwest of Moravian Falls, the areas along US 421 east and west of Wilkesboro, and the areas by the outlying communities of Thurmond, Austin, and Clingman.

As with other elements of the plan, these designated areas are rather general due to the map scale and to provide a variety of site possibilities for the 900 additional acres projected. Existing industry is also represented in some cases. It should be pointed out that in seeking desirable industry, both design and performance standards (noise, smoke, dust, odors, etc.) should be considered. Zoning ordinances as well as restrictive covenants (by private landowners) can help insure that industrial growth is in keeping with desirable standards.

FORESTRY, RECREATION AND
CONSERVATION ELEMENT

This portion of proposed future land use is by far the largest due to the forestry portion involved. The recreation and conservation areas are so closely related to forestry that they are included here. Each of the three major elements will be discussed separately.

Forestry

Wilkes County has about 365,000 acres of forest land that can be harvested and replenished by either commercial or individual operations. (Not included in this figure are the "public" lands such as the Federally reserved areas along the Blue Ridge Parkway or around the W. Kerr Scott Reservoir.)

The future land use projections indicated that this forestry land will be decreased only slightly during the planning period to 1990. As shown on the land development plan, this wooded land is spread across the Brushy Mountains in the southern portion of the county and from west to north along the Blue Ridge Mountains.

Areas with common forestry, recreation and conservation delineations are in the northern part of the county, around the proposed Reddies River Reservoir and Roaring River Reservoir, and along the major rivers.

It was pointed out in Part I of this report that the forestry areas offer a good source of income and that there is ample room to improve this income through proper management and marketing practices. It is to the advantage of the landowner and county alike to encourage good forestry practices which serve to improve the economic benefits of the land while preserving the scenie and recreational benefits of the county as well.

Recreation

The future land use projection for public, semi-public land for use in Wilkes County by 1990 was for 1,140 additional acres. This acreage would be largely for recreational purposes since most governmental buildings and similar such uses within this public, semi-public category are likely to be within the central Wilkesboro-North Wilkesboro area and were thus not included in the projection for additional land for this use.

Some basic principles to be considered in locating recreation sites are as follows:

-- A wide variety of areas and facilities should be provided to meet the needs of all ages, regarless of economic status or race.
-- Various parts of the county should be provided with centrally located areas that are as convenient to as many users as possible.

-- Natural features of the county that are particularly
   suited for recreational use should be preserved for
   public use.

-- Areas chosen for recreational use should be protected
   from safety hazards, from neighboring uses that might
   not be compatible, and the recreational use should be
   so located and arranged that it causes the least
   possible bad effects on the surrounding neighborhood.

-- Recreation areas should be attractive, and provide
   sufficient space for safety and proper design.

The largest recreation area delineated on the land development
plan map includes the Little Grandfather Wildlife Management Area
and the Blue Ridge Parkway Recreational Area (Doughton Park), both
in the northern part of the county. Because of the terrain and
scenic attraction of this area, the land should be left largely
in its natural state. Such activities could be provided: picnicking, hiking, riding, hunting and fishing, camping, and at least
some play equipment for small children. Picnicking and camping
facilities are now provided in Doughton Park, and hunting and
fishing are allowed in the Little Grandfather (Thurmond Chatham)
Wildlife Management Area at certain times during the year. Additional equipment could be added for the activities mentioned without detracting from the general appearance and other features of
the land.

The second largest area delineated on the map for recreational
use is the land in the vicinity of Stone Mountain, in the north-
eastern portion of the county along the Wilkes-Alleghany County
line. This large mass of gray granite and some 3,000 acres of the
surrounding land has been approved by the North Carolina Conservation and Development Board for addition to the State park system.
State and Federal representatives are currently working together
to finance and develop the park. This facility should include
natural areas (for hiking, riding, scenis views, etc.), more
formally developed areas (for swimming, golfing, tennis, etc.),
and commercial areas (such as restaurants, craft shops, service

to motorists, and possibly motel facilities). Such a park with widespread activities would not only provide recreation for local residents, but would be a good tourist attraction for the county and region.

Another possibility for the urban type recreation activities mentioned above would be the areas indicated in the vicinity of the proposed Reddies River Reservoir. Being so close to the population center of the county around the Wilkesboros, Millers Creek, Cricket, Mulberry and Fairplains, this flood control project would also provide an excellent opportunity for a county recreation facility for all ages. Besides the fishing and water sports that will be offered, land should be acquired through the combined efforts of the county, state and federal governments for such active uses as playfields for baseball and other outdoor games, playgrounds for various ages, tennis, etc. There would also be room for less urban type activities (hiking, riding, nature trails, etc.) at both this and the proposed Roaring River Reservoir to the east of North Wilkesboro.

Several semi-natural park areas in the county are indicated on the land development plan. These include:

-- Rendezvous Mountain -- a topographic and legendary attraction in west Wilkes that is already state-owned and offers good potential for several of the activities previously discussed;

-- Wells Knob -- a small but scenic feature of nature in northeast Wilkes;

-- Fitches Knob -- another prominent landmark on NC 115 in the southeast; and

-- Attractive sites along the Yadkin River, near Ronda, and Warrior Creek, west of Boomer. The latter features a scenic waterfall that has gone unnoticed by most residents of the area heretofore.

Commercial recreation possibilities are many -- as indicated
in the Land Potential portion of this report. Two possible areas
for large commercial recreation activities (ski lodges, summer
camps, outdoor drama, amusement center, etc.) are delineated along
the Blue Ridge Parkway in west Wilkes. Additional possibilities
that are not delineated include commercial development on the
existing W. Kerr Scott Reservoir and the proposed Reddies River
and Roaring River reservoirs, as well as numerous possible locations for skeet and trap shooting ranges and similar ventures
that could be provided in almost any of the less densely developed
portions of the county. Also not delineated are the existing stock
car racing and drag racing commercial facilities and numerous areas
that would provide adequate room for the expansion of these and other
spectator sports.

Conservation

The conservation delineations of the plan are primarily
stream basins and flood plains. They include the land along the
Yadkin River, Stony Fork Creek and Lewis Fork Creek (west of
Champion), Warrior Creek and Moravian Creek (west of Moravian
Falls), Reddies River and Mulberry Creek (north of North Wilkesboro), Roaring River and its tributaries, and Hunting Creek in the
southeast. One exception to the areas subject to flooding or wetness is the large conservation area delineated between Doughton
Park and Stone Mountain. This land is largely steep and stony and
does not lend itself to most uses which would change it from its
natural state.

It is suggested that these areas be left in a natural state,
and development there be discouraged. Other purposes could be
served, however, such as forestry and recreation. With good management practices forestry would support conservation and not cause
erosion or pollution along the streams. The natural state would
promote wildlife propagation and make good recreational use in the
form of hunting and fishing.

59

Another designation on the plan under conservation is the historic site proposal. There are four: the Roundabout (home place of Ben Cleveland) near Ronda, the cabin of Cleveland's brother near Purlear, and Boone's cabin and Tom Dula's grave, both of which are near Ferguson. Immediate action should be taken by the county to arrange financing to obtain these and the natural recreation sites that were mentioned in the previous section (Wells Knob, Fitches Knob, and the scenic waterfall area on Warrior Creek). It is very possible that private funds and gifts would be provided in some cases if this matter were promoted. Increased tourism is another side effect that could result from these historical and recreational site preservation efforts.

One further consideration is the need for seeding or surfacing areas that are disturbed in the course of urban-type development. Land that is cleared for roads, subdivisions, and industrial or commercial construction will quickly erode with the topography that is present. The United States Department of Agriculture's Soil Conservation Service offers valuable assistance here. Requirements for such surface cover should be strongly emphasized in connection with all future plans for urban development.

Thoroughfare Plan

Wilkes County is experiencing some problems now as a result of more and faster traffic, as was pointed in the Land Potential section of this report. It is only logical to believe that as the county population and developed areas increase in the future, the county road system must be improved to meet the demand of more traffic. Planning as far in advance as possible for these improvements will help to make the roads safer and more pleasant to travel. Other benefits of thoroughfare planning that relate to all citizens either directly or indirectly are listed below, as outlined by the Advance Planning Department of the State Highway Commission:

PROPOSED
ETCH THOROUGHFARE PLAN
Source: N.C. Highway Commission

LEGEND

	EXISTING	PROPOSED
PRIMARY HIGHWAYS		
MAJOR COUNTY ROADS		
ALTERNATE MAJOR COUNTY ROADS		

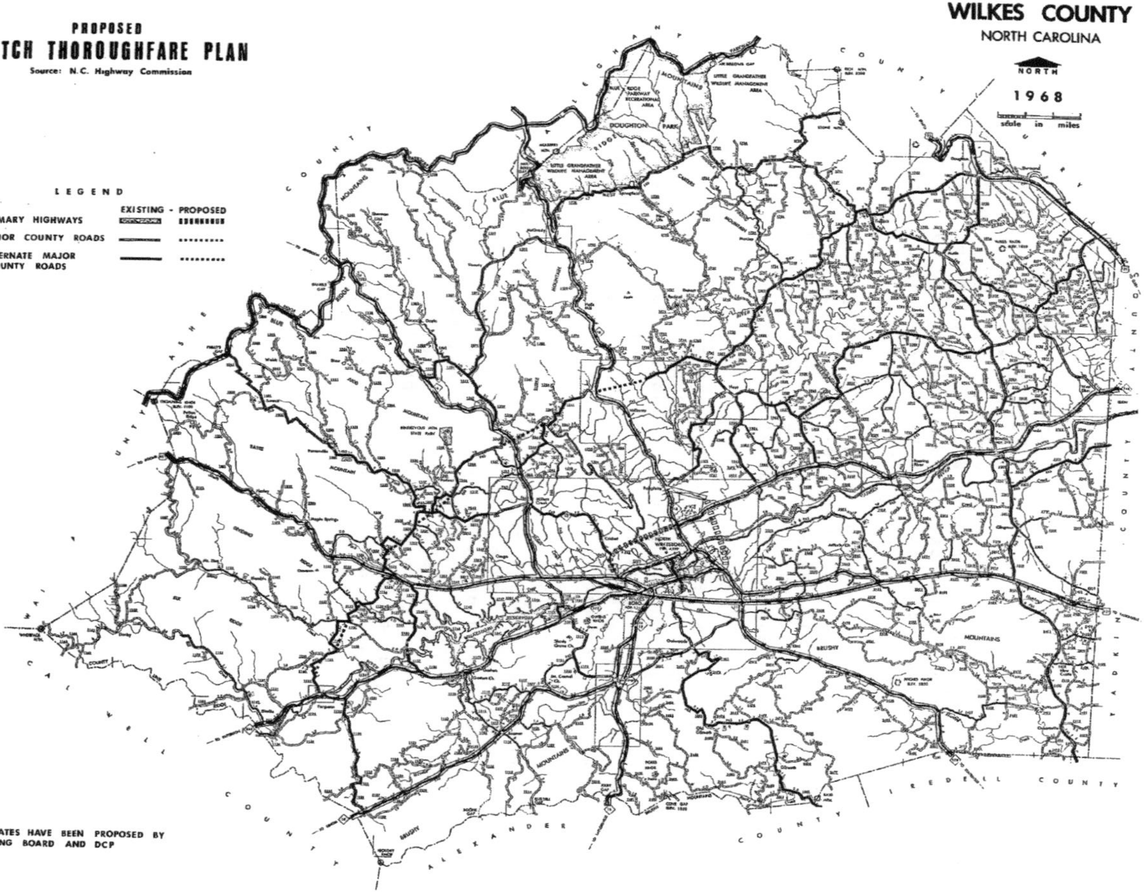

WILKES COUNTY
NORTH CAROLINA

NORTH

1968

scale in miles

TE:
SENATES HAVE BEEN PROPOSED BY
ANNING BOARD AND DCP

MAP-11

1. U.S. 421. This east-west route across the county will no
    doubt have increasing importance to the county and region
    during the planning period (to 1990). The bypass route
    shown passing south of the Wilkesboros as existing road-
    way is under construction and should be completed by 1969.
    It is recommended that the western portion of this road
    (from Champion to the Wilkes-Watauga County line) be
    improved to the same level as the eastern and bypass
    portions.

2. N.C. 268. This important regional route is heavily
    travelled in the eastern portion of the county and traffic
    should increase, particularly with the anticipated devel-
    opment in the counties immediately to the east of Wilkes.
    A bypass to the north of the Wilkesboros on this road is
    included as a part of the North Wilkesboro-Wilkesboro
    Thoroughfare Plan. This bypass should be implemented as
    early as possible, and should be closely coordinated with
    the proposed U.S. Corps of Engineers project of the
    Reddies River Reservoir which is to be in the area of the
    bypass. The remainder of this road (both east and west
    from the Wilkesboros) should be widened and improved to
    accommodate the increasing traffic anticipated later in
    the planning period.

3. N.C. 16. This north-south route has been greatly im-
    proved from the southern county line to Wilkesboro and
    by the new alignment from U.S. 421 to Millers Creek.
    This type of improvement should be extended from Millers
    Creek to the Blue Ridge Parkway, an important access into
    the county for tourists and other traffic from the Blue
    Ridge Mountains.

4. N.C. 18. This north-south route will become more impor-
    tant to the county as the land development Plan is imple-
    mented due to its relation to proposed recreation areas,
    the Stone Mountain Park area, and the Blue Ridge Parkway.
    It is recommended that it be widened and realigned across
    the county.

5. N.C. 21. This heavily travelled route across the north-
    east corner of the county will also receive more traffic
    with the advent of the Stone Mountain Park. It is
    recommended that it be improved where it leaves Wilkes
    County and across a portion of Alleghany County to the
    Blue Ridge Parkway to give a better access to the eastern
    side of the Stone Mountain area.

6. **N.C. 115.** This route should gain in importance during the planning period as a link with the Western Piedmont Crescent portion of the state. The North Wilkesboro-Wilkesboro Thoroughfare Plan includes a bypass on this route to the east of North Wilkesboro. This bypass should be implemented to serve the industrial development and other traffic needs here where the traffic count in 1966 was the highest in the county (Map 6). The remainder of this road should be improved to handle the heavier traffic anticipated during the latter portion of the planning period.

Major County Roads. These facilities interconnect economic, population, and recreational centers within the county and adjacent counties and carry traffic to the primary highway system. They are generally continuous and serve areas of considerable size.

1. **SR 1002.** This route is probably the most important road of this category since it is serving almost as a primary highway for the northeast sector of the county. It is heavily travelled and there is no doubt that traffic will be increased considerably with the development of the Stone Mountain Park and other development that will result from favorable factors in this portion of the county. It is recommended that this road be upgraded and rerouted as necessary to eliminate several sharp, narrow curves that exist along its present alignment. This improvement should be undertaken along the entire route, from Fairplains to Doughton.

2. **McGrady to Traphill.** This route will also be closely related to the Stone Mountain Park and other recreational areas proposed by the land development plan. The county routes of SR 1728, SR 1730, SR 1737, and SR 1739 (leading from the Joynes community to Stone Mountain) should be improved and maintained as a scenic greenway with limited traffic (no trucks) to provide an attractive access to the park and recreation complex. Much of this route leading from McGrady along the wildlife management area in northern Wilkes has been recently realigned and paved through normal county maintenance, and this treatment should be extended as rapidly as possible to provide better access to the Stone Mountain area.

3. <u>Hays to Ferguson</u>. This route is suggested as an additional route to the plan proposed by State Highway Advance Planning Department (Map 11). Once completed, it would be an important factor in the county's land development plan, as it would link such important points as the one existing and two proposed reservoirs, the Rendezvous Mountain State Park, and proposed historic sites. The alternate route suggested would utilize existing roadbeds in most cases, with some realignment and widening of present hazardous sections.

4. <u>SR 1150 to SR 1137</u>. This crossing on the western end of the W. Kerr Scott Reservoir was proposed earlier in the <u>Future Land Use Plan for Wilkesboro, North Wilkesboro and Wilkes County</u> (Division of Community Planning, 1962). It would link the two primary highways in this portion of the county (U.S. 421 and N.C. 268), would save considerable driving distance around the reservoir, and would help greatly in opening this prime residential land to development.

5. <u>Other Major County Roads</u>. Further review of Map 11 will reveal additional roads proposed as major county toads throughout the county. These roads serve most of the remaining portions of the county and in most cases link other major county roads and primary highway routes. Included on the map are the Hays to N.C. 21 route, with connectors to N.C. 268; a north-south route in the eastern part of the county, connecting Doughton, Austin, Ronda, Clingman, and the Somers Township area of the county; SR 1001, which is a connector with Alexander and Iredell Counties to the south; SR 1129, 1130, and 1132, which together form a connector between N.C. 18 and N.C. 268 in the southwest part of the county; and finally, SR 1300 and SR 1575, which serve the Blue Ridge Mountain area between U.S. 421 and N.C. 16, and between N.C. 16 and N.C. 18. As with most of the roads mentioned previously, these various routes should be scheduled for widening and realignment in most cases to better handle increasing traffic. It is recommended, however, that these improvements be scheduled after those listed under Primary Highways and Major County Roads above.

Naturally, the Wilkes County Thoroughfare Plan should be coordinated with the land development plan. The extension of utility systems, and other major improvements. This not only tends to prevent costly repairs of roads that must be opened for underground lines and pipes, but a new or improved road in itself is often the needed incentive for property owners to improve the general appearance of their property. Coupled with a coordinated plan for a sizable area, roads can be an important tool for plan implementation. Other tools are discussed in the following section on implementation.

part 4

PART IV

IMPLEMENTATION

This land development plan for Wilkes County cannot serve its
intended purpose as a guide for the future unless it is implemented.
There are several tools available for this process, some of which
are in use in the county and some that should be added. Implementation tools and recommendations for their use in Wilkes County are
listed below, followed by a recommended implementation program.

IMPLEMENTATION TOOLS

ZONING -- This tool allows the County Board of Commissioners
to regulate private development within the county or
certain parts of it. The existing zoning ordinance
can be broadened and revised in accordance with the
comprehensive plan for the county. The county has
zoning in force for the W. Kerr Scott Reservoir area,
and the County Planning Board is studying additional
areas which will be recommended to the Board of
Commissioners for zoning at a later date.

It is recommended that the Wilkes County Commissioners
employ a full-time administrator for this program and
support him in every needful way.

SUBDIVISION REGULATIONS -- These regulations set standards
for lots, roads, building setbacks, the drawing of
plats, etc., in regard to land to be subdivided for
residential use. Wilkes County was brought under the
protection of subdivision regulations enacted in 1961.

It is recommended that these regulations be strictly
administered.

BUILDING AND HOUSING CODES -- These legal codes (including
electrical and plumbing codes) insure safe and sound
building construction. They can be enacted to apply
to new and remodeling construction and to old buildings as well.

It is recommended that the North Carolina Uniform Residential Building Code, as amended, be adopted by the Wilkes County Board of Commissioners and steps taken to enforce this and the North Carolina Building Code (unless the Board of Commissioners prefers to have a code drafted and enact this in lieu of the North Carolina codes).

PUBLIC IMPROVEMENTS PROGRAM -- This program scheduled capital improvements over a long period of time. Many advantages result from such planning for these improvements -- such as the ability to maintain a fairly steady tax rate (rather than raising the rate when something is critically needed), a strong county financial system and credit standing is maintained, and public confidence is inspired in the governing body and administrative officials. County officials should start working toward a public improvements program that is based on the land development plan and revised from time to time as the need arises.

CITIZEN PARTICIPATION -- This is probably the most important implementation tool listed. An informed public is more willing to support growth and development programs whether in their neighborhood or in the county. Wilkes County officials should begin immediately to see that the public is informed about planning efforts. A major step in this direction would be the formal adoption of the land development plan after holding a public hearing on it by the Board of Commissioners.

OTHER TOOLS -- Not all of the means for plan implementation can be listed here. Many federal programs are available for major county projects such as FHA grants for water and sewer facilities. Other programs that should be investigated include assistance involving Building and Housing Code Enforcement, Community Renewal Programs, Rural Renewal Programs, Solid Waste (garbage) Disposal Facilities, and Open Space Land Acquisition for Parks, Conservation and Historic Properties. Aid from private groups should be enlisted also, such as community development organizations, school boards, and farm and home demonstration groups -- all of which could provide much help in implementing portions of the overall plan in their particular locality. Private enterprise should be requested to help county planning efforts in reference to such developments as shopping centers, mobile home parks, and industrial parks.

RECOMMENDED IMPLEMENTATION PROGRAM

To relate more specifically some of the tools for implementation with the land development plan for Wilkes County, the
following recommendations are given. Short-range has reference
to items that can be accomplished in the first one to six years
of the planning period. Long-range items would be completed in
the remaining part of the planning period.

Residential Element

Short-Range

1. Enlist interest in the land development plan from the
   public by publicizing it through news media and holding public hearings on it, followed by formal adoption
   by the County Board of Commissioners. Civic and other
   volunteer groups should be informed of the overall planning efforts and asked to help with its promotion as a
   long-range goal.

2. Enactment of additional zoning coverage as recommended
   by the County Planning Board, including a full-time
   administrator.

3. Establish county policy on garbage dumping and set up
   landfills or other necessary operations to reduce the
   existing problem of many scattered dumps.

4. Enactment of building and housing codes to insure
   sound new construction and upgrade older buildings.

5. Better housing is needed for many Wilkes County citizens. A County Housing Authority should be considered,
   although a change in the present N. C. General Statutes
   would be necessary since counties under 60,000 in population are not now permitted to establish such author-
   ities. A Housing Authority would make it possible to
   use Federal loans to purchase, remodel and rent existing housing as public housing units for low-income
   families. New housing units could be built through a
   housing authority, or by churches and other nonprofit
   organizations which are also eligible for Federal loans
   for construction of low rent housing.

6. Set up administrative machinery for a Public Improvements Program, including additional water and sewer services, based on heavier population growth areas proposed in the land development plan, recommendations from the engineering study in progress, and from the Public Facilities Plan.

Long-Range

1. Further extension of zoned areas to protect growing urban-residential and rural-neighborhood residential areas.

2. Schedule additional capital improvements in Public Improvements Program based on land development plan, public facilities plan, and growth trends.

3. Continue planning program to update physical plans to meet growth needs, and to assist officials in anticipating these needs as far in advance as possible.

AGRICULTURAL AND RURAL RESIDENTIAL ELEMENT

Short-Range

1. Enact zoning to protect agricultural land from rampant speculation and undesirable growth effects.

2. Enlist leaders in rural communities in efforts to improve housing conditions, local economic and education levels, and local recreational facilities. Improvement in these local communities could be promoted through such programs as (FHA) Rural Renewal Loans and Rural Housing Loans, and through Community Action Programs of the Office of Economic Opportunity.

3. Coordinate county physical planning with agricultural, soil and other agencies to promote overall community development and conservation of land.

Long-Range

1. Continue to implement major county road improvements, working with the North Carolina Highway Commission and including financial plans for this in the county Public Improvements Program.

2. Continue efforts toward community betterment through coordination of land management and environmental improvement programs of county, state, and federal agencies.

FORESTRY, RECREATION AND CONSERVATION ELEMENT

Short-Range

1. Begin acquisition of potential recreation sites through private efforts, a recreation commission, possible Federal assistance through the Open-Space Land Program, or a combination of these efforts -- particularly in areas where historic or outstanding natural features exist.

2. Give particular attention to these areas for protection of forests and conservation resources through zoning.

3. Commercial recreation ventures should be encouraged and aided by county government when in keeping with the land development plan and overall county improvement. This may be accomplished through long-term leasing of public property to individuals, or firms, federal cost-sharing, or state-county assistance -- and may require special legislation in some cases. Such efforts could mean much to the county, both in economic and recreational benefits.

4. Implement the McGrady to Traphill portion of the thoroughfare plan to improve access to the proposed Stone Mountain Park area.

Long-Range

1. Continue acquisition efforts for land of prime recreational areas, particularly in the vicinity of the Reddies River and Roaring River flood control projects, the Stone Mountain Park area, and such natural features as waterfalls or mountains.

2. Establish a recreation commission or recreation department and set up a supervised county recreation program. Arrange financing for this program, including a special tax vote, if necessary, to provide funds for varied activities for all ages.

71

INDUSTRIAL AND COMMERCIAL ELEMENT

Short-Range

1. Reserve prime industrial land through zoning, and by obtaining options on property through a development commission or other group set up to promote industrial development.

2. Emphasize desirable standards in new industrial development through zoning requirements and encouragement of private landowners' use of restrictive covenants.

3. Encourage compact commercial development through sound zoning procedures to discourage scattered, strip development along major roads.

4. Promote commercial recreation and tourism through a development commission (or "tourism commission") to seek this type of activity for the county. With proper promotion this type of "industry" could be greatly increased.

Long-Range

1. Continue to emphasize conservation of water, forests, and other natural resources in industrial and commercial growth through zoning and encouraging cooperation from private developers.

2. Promote better income levels countywide through expanded use of industrial education facilities by residents from all communities. This increased education and training will encourage more diversified industrial development with more job opportunities.

3. Update the land development plan and zoning from time to time to keep pace with growth trends in regards to additional commercial areas to complement residential and industrial development.

THOROUGHFARE PLAN

Short-Range

1. Adopt plans in conjunction with the Advance Planning
    Department of the Highway Commission concerning
    countywide transportation.

2. Begin implementation as early as possible of SR 1002
    improvement in the northeastern part of the county.

3. Proceed with early implementation of the McGrady to
    Traphill route. This link will be important to the
    development and use of the Stone Mountain Park area.

4. Complete the North Wilkesboro-Wilkesboro Thoroughfare
    Plan bypasses (N.C. 268 and N.C. 115) to provide better
    traffic flow across the county.

5. Promote (through neighborhood groups, civic organiza-
    tions, etc.) community beautification along with the
    improvement of the rural county roads. (Local interest
    in other improvements will be heightened as new or
    improved roads are completed.)

Long-Range

1. Further implementation of the thoroughfare plan, both
    of the primary highways and major county roads.

2. Include thoroughfares in updating of plans to best
    serve developing residential, commercial, industrial
    and recreational areas.

REDDIES RIVER RESERVOIR
REDDIES RIVER, NORTH CAROLINA

Source: North Carolina
          Department of Water & Air Resources

APPENDIX B

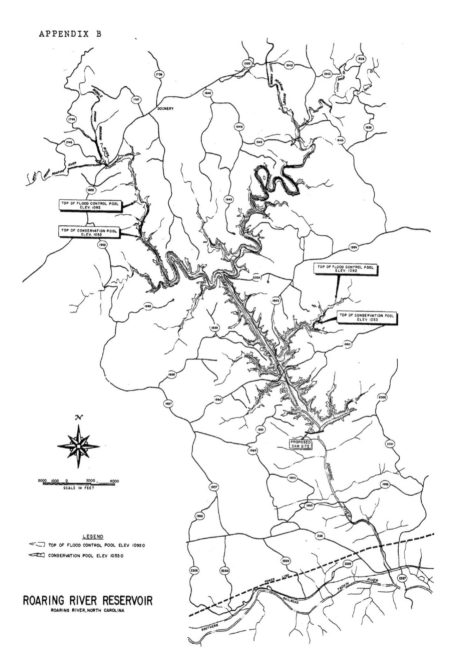

LEGEND

TOP OF FLOOD CONTROL POOL ELEV 1092.0

CONSERVATION POOL ELEV 1053.0

ROARING RIVER RESERVOIR
ROARING RIVER, NORTH CAROLINA

Source: North Carolina
         Department of Water & Air Resources

Lightning Source UK Ltd.
Milton Keynes UK
UKHW021904121118
332198UK00014B/293/P